PROJECT MANAGEMENT BATTLEFIELD

PROJECT MANAGEMENT BATTLEFIELD

Sun Tzu's wisdom on project management

Book One – Warrior's Quest

PUNEET KUTHIALA

The Project Management Battlefield
Sun Tzu's wisdom on project management
Book I – Warrior's Quest

by Puneet Kuthiala

Copyright © 2013 Puneet Kuthiala. All rights reserved.

ISBN: 148023236X
ISBN-13: 9781480232365

PMBOK, PMP are copyrights of PMI, USA
The Art of War is adopted from Project Gutenberg

Contents

Acknowledgments 2

About This Book 4

How To Read This Book 6

Forward 8

PART I 10

    CHAPTER 1 The Comparison 11

    CHAPTER 2 The General 15

    CHAPTER 3 The Environment 30

    CHAPTER 4 Project Integration Management 37

    CHAPTER 5 Project Scope Management 48

    CHAPTER 6 Project Time Management 60

    CHAPTER 7 Project Cost Management 71

    CHAPTER 8 Project Quality Management 78

    CHAPTER 9 Project Human Resource Management 85

    CHAPTER 10 Project Communications Management 96

    CHAPTER 11 Project Risk Management 106

    CHAPTER 12 Project Procurement Management 124

    CHAPTER 13 Beyond PMBOK® 130

PART II 140

    CHAPTER 14 Laying Plans 142

    CHAPTER 15 Waging War 145

    CHAPTER 16 Attack By Stratagem 148

    CHAPTER 17 Tactical Dispositions 151

    CHAPTER 18 Energy 153

    CHAPTER 19 Weak Points And Strong Points 156

    CHAPTER 20 Maneuvering 160

    CHAPTER 21 Variation In Tactics 164

    CHAPTER 22 The Army On The March 166

    CHAPTER 23 Terrain 171

    CHAPTER 24 The Nine Situations 176

    CHAPTER 25 The Attack By Fire 184

    CHAPTER 26 The Use Of Spies 187

Afterward 191

To all my professional colleagues,

Each and every one of them has contributed to this book.

Past, present, and future!

Acknowledgments

Nothing is created alone.

All of us are familiar with the stories of the greatest inventors in the world. Often, through these stories, we come to believe that the inventions and innovations are a single person's work. Most of the time the invention encompasses more than what meets the eye. A creative piece of work takes more effort in sustaining and supporting the process of creation than the very act of creation. An idea needs a multitude of thoughts, actions, and a support system in its journey to manifestation.

Nothing is created alone. That is the case with this book.

I could not have done it alone.

First things first. In over a decade of working in the technology industry, I had the fortune of working with several professionals. Working with each one of them has resulted in an accumulation of insights and knowledge. Had it not been for the years of communication, collaboration, and cooperation of my coworkers, it wouldn't have been possible to gain any insights into the profession.

Sony Gabriel, has helped me greatly during the initial research on this project, and he did more than I asked him to do.

Although no creation is produced alone, the process of creation makes one lonely. One has to let the process absorb oneself. I experienced frequent lost-in-thought moments during the writing of this book. There were times when I found myself daydreaming about the battlefields and the actions of the general. At times, these wandering thoughts revealed similarities between *The Art of War*

Acknowledgments

and PMBOK® while I sat at the dinner table, without realizing I should have been giving my family some good company. During the writing of this book, there were occasions when I woke up with general-like thoughts. For many days, I simply forgot the world around me. My daily life, routine, and work went ahead, undisturbed.

I am thankful to my wife, Shaloo, and my daughter, Saruha. They are the pillars upon whom this work was built.

About This Book

Working in a project environment, one needs to interact and collaborate with others. Each of such interaction opens up an opportunity to learn and explore the world around us. The learning we pick up is greatly influenced by the values, cultural orientations, and perceptions of the world in which we have lived.

This book is for project managers, beginners, experienced professionals, and veterans of the subject. *The Art of War* offers a depth of knowledge and insights that can benefit the community and can help a great deal to understand the world in which we work. I am introducing *The Art of War* to the project managers through this book.

The Art of War – Sun Tzu

The Art of War is a military treatise written by Sun Tzu, who was a veteran of the army, who oversaw many victories and helped forge an empire. Sun Tzu, who is believed to have lived during the fifth century BC, wrote this "manual" on wooden plates for the generals. *The Art of War* is a short book of just thirteen chapters, each chapter focuses on one or another topic concerning war. Each of the chapters consists of a few statements that are related to the topic, and Sun Tzu advises a general and sometime the head of the state on the different aspects of conduct during war.

Though this text was known even to the common people in the region of China, it was discovered by the western world in the eighteenth century. The first translation was in French, and later on it was translated by many people around the world. *The Art of War* is a military classic, in modern times, it has contributed to a great amount of literature and thought in the management sciences. While researching this book, I came across many versions and finally, used what I thought was the best version of the book. Section II of this book is a free copy of *The Art of War* for the reader's benefit.

The Art of War is known as a "manual" for an army general.

Project Management Body of Knowledge – Project Management Institute

A Guide to the Project Management Body of Knowledge (PMBOK®) is a globally recognized book that set standard processes, terminology, and guidelines for use while managing projects. First published as a white paper by the Project Management Institute (PMI) in 1983. PMBOK®, as a book and a detail guide, was first published in 1996, and the most recent fourth edition was published in 2008. At the time writing, the fifth edition was planned to be released in early 2013. This comparison is based on the fourth edition of PMBOK®.

Since then, PMI's approach has become a defacto standard for project managers and organizations. While professionals with knowledge of these standards remain a respected lot, the evidence is mounting that these standards also help organizations deliver results that are aligned with their strategic objectives. I frequently refer to this book as a "manual" for project managers.

This is a book of comparison of the intent of *The Art of War* with that of the PMBOK® and has great deal of instances where *The Art of War* can offer deep knowledge, insights and ideas to the project management community.

How to Read This Book

This book is about the similarities between the world's two most famous manuals: *The Art of War* and PMBOK®, and it will appeal to readers regardless of their experience.

Section one is about similarities between PMBOK® and *The Art of War* and also discusses, though briefly, ideas and concepts that are not covered in PMBOK® but are of great benefit for a project manager.

Section two is the reader's free copy of *The Art of War*.

Some of the elements in *The Art of War* can be found to have a direct meaning in PMBOK®, and some of them do not, they offer some key learning nevertheless. Therefore, for the benefit of the reader, I have added a dedicated section for notes, where the readers can take notes.

A free, electronic copy of *The Art of War* is also available on request. Please contact me at aow@puneetkuthiala.com with subject Art of War.

Reader's familiarity with PMBOK® will help him to get maximum out of this book, however, for readers' benefit, a brief overview of the PMBOK® is described in the following paragraph.

PMBOK® describes processes that are needed in the project management Lifecycle. The project management Lifecycle is the journey of the project from Project Initiation, Project Planning, Project Execution, Project Control and finally to Project Closure. There are a variety of processes, tools, techniques and controls that are needed while managing the project through each of the above mentioned Lifecycle stages. These processes are structured in nine knowledge areas as follows – Project Integration Management, Project Scope Management, Project Time Management, Project Cost Management, Project Quality Management, Project Human Resource Management, Project Communications Management, Project Risk Management, and Project Procurement Management. For easy reading, Section one is structured similar to the knowledge areas - Chapter 4 to Chapter 12 are titled with the appropriate knowledge areas' name.

In each of the chapters, the comparison follows an easy to understand format. It begins with chapter title from *The Art of War*, in bold and capital letters, followed by the quotations from *The Art of War*, in bullets (→), and their application to the project management comes at the end, which appears in italics in a box.

Get Involved

As you read these two books, the similarities between them become clearer, and it is very likely that the reader's understanding and perspectives about PMBOK® in comparison with *The Art of War* will bring additional thoughts and ideas to the table.

Readers can send their feedback, ideas and their own interpretation of *The Art of War* at battlefield@puneetkuthiala.com.

Forward

This is a book about quests.

The intent of *The Art of War* was to give a structured methodology to army generals to enable them to deliver positive outcomes on the battlefield. *The Art of War* was meant for generals who had completed their basic education and had battlefield experience.

I was introduced to PMBOK® in 2003 while studying for my Project Management Professional (PMP®) certification exam. I did very well and passed the exam. I first read *The Art of War* in my early twenties, but if had there been an exam based on this book, I would have done miserably as I had understood almost nothing.

On a cold, dull, dark winter day of early 2012, I was listening to the audio version of this military classic on my way home from work and was listening to it passively. The entire text by Sun Tzu focused on guiding the general toward a positive outcome, by cluing into the environment in which he operates. It intrigued me. The entire philosophy in PMBOK® also revolves around a similar intention. A project manager must strive to deliver, via his team, an outcome that is accepted by all stakeholders, making it a win-win for all of them. A project manager necessarily has to ensure that the project continues to contribute to the business objectives, to keep adding value to the stakeholders' interests, and hence to help the organization gain market share.

The similarity was striking and deserved more analysis, which made me ponder my own work experiences. As I had slowly grown in experience, I noticed that we live in a world that depends on positive outcomes. I couldn't fail to notice that the metamorphosis of the "war" had occurred. The marketplace, in my mind, had been transformed into a battlefield. On every project I had the opportunity to work on, I had to work harder and perform better for the success that helped the organizations outpace the competition. The battle was no longer for territory. The organizations were battling for growth in market share. The organizations strived for positive outcomes through various strategies. I saw the wars in creating products and services that a consumer would buy, thereby increasing market share in a competitive marketplace.

As a quality management and project management professional, I have helped projects deliver within constraints. The Positive Outcome has become my defining principle in selecting an execution approach for any given project. The same is true with my approach to this book.

After spending a few weeks comparing the two books, I found that their similarities are abundant and worth sharing with the rest of the community in the form of a book. There is a wealth of knowledge that a project manager can gather and apply in his work.

PMBOK® is a proponent of a methodical and process-oriented approach. Interpretation of this book is uniform in the industry. *The Art of War* is a prescription and a methodology intended for generals. It was written more than 2500 years ago. The guidelines provided in this document are for army generals. Interpretations of these guidelines for the project management world will vary among individuals, based on their cultural backgrounds, experiences, and thinking orientations.

The fundamental message is same in the both the texts: avoid conflicts to win wars (markets).

SECTION I
The Comparison

CHAPTER 1

The Comparison

While writing this book, many similarities were found between the two texts. The intent of the processes described in PMBOK® has similarities with the statements found in *The Art of War* by Sun Tzu. While I had a tough time in comparing procurement management with *The Art of War*, the two texts have a similar approach though subject matters are different. *The Art of War* speaks a great deal about the personal skills of the general, someone who might be a project manager in our world, an aspect that is discussed briefly in PMBOK®. Moreover, there were a few ideas and statements in *The Art of War* that were not touched on in PMBOK® that I think would greatly benefit a project manager in managing projects.

The project manager can benefit from many of the strategic and tactical principles outlined in this military classic. *The Art of War* is a guide to anticipating and overcoming obstacles. *The Art of War* is more about strategy than describing ways to win battles, and many ideas from it can be adopted to improve the chances of a positive outcome in business and to reduce the chances of failure.

Most of the messages in *The Art of War* are efforts to anticipate and overcome obstacles, the obstacles that have the potential to stop you from achieving success. According to *The Art of War*, managing threats should be first and foremost in the minds of generals in every battle. With teachings of *The Art of War*, the general can manage the threats in various stages of the battle.

Similarly, in PMBOK®, risk management is a very important aspect of project management.

According to Sun Tzu in *The Art of War*, a general should aim to win the battle as efficiently as possible within the constraints. The emphasis in *The Art of War* is on being efficient in the use of resources to achieve results. Sun Tzu places importance on winning battles with minimal costs. Some statements in the book have direct implications on the cost of waging a war. In PMBOK®, the goal of the manager is not just to get the work done, but to get it done as efficiently as possible given the limited resources he can have. It is the project manager's job to evaluate what must be done and plan the best possible use of the resources available to him. The emphasis in PMBOK® is not just about the successful project's implementation but about meeting the project expectations within the defined constraints of cost, time, and quality.

Dependency of a project's outcome, on the enterprise environmental factors, internal and external dependencies are a few of the repeating themes in PMBOK®. Sun Tzu also emphasizes their importance and says that environment plays an important role in a project's success. Success does not go always to the strongest or the most aggressive, but to those who best understand their situation and the various alternatives available to them.

In *The Art of War*, Sun Tzu places emphasis on strategy in battles. In war, a positive outcome depends on the positions and movements — the positions that enemies cannot attack and movements that he cannot detect. While PMBOK® emphasizes planning, there is an element of strategy in discussion of continuous process improvement, management of risks to avoid threats, and exploitation of threats to help organizations mature. The strategy around the threats and their exploitation helps in gaining consumer confidence and market share.

The Art of War directs a general to avoid conflicts because conflict is seen as inherently costly. It also teaches how to handle direct, hostile confrontations when they cannot be avoided. The general is advised to be proactive in his approach to defuse these situations before they occur. The emphasis is on establishing the proper communication channels. In PMBOK® also, the emphasis is to avoid conflicts as much as possible by proactive actions and via proper communication mechanisms in the team. Communication is the aspect that defines the success or failure in projects.

Teamwork is the lifeline of all the organizations. Be it a modern organization or any state during ancient times, both can fall or rise with teamwork in action. Both the texts also place a great importance on this aspect of humans. While Sun Tzu links success in battle directly to the ability to collaborate, communicate, and act as a cohesive team, in the battlefield, PMBOK® also stresses the importance of communicating and collaborating between members of teams. Both texts emphasize the importance of leaders encouraging the development of strong teams and creating the necessary environment for improving team bonding. Rewards and recognition are also emphasized in both books.

While PMBOK® enlists some tools necessary for quality management, like benchmarking that assist a project manager in assessing project situations, Sun Tzu has also emphasized that a general should understand deficiencies and plan according to the "need" of the outcome. In *The Art of War*, the need for quality control and strict adherence to quality is also emphasized to ensure the positions are made unassailable during war.

While scope management is unarguably a topic expected to be discussed in PMBOK®, in *The Art of War*, adequate references to the importance of scope are also found, wherein Sun Tzu discusses the importance of knowing what needs to be accomplished in a war that would help a general to ensure victory. Similarly, *The*

Art of War also puts emphasis on estimation, activity sequencing, and resource allocation—just what we expect in Project Time Management.

Due to the very nature of the topic, *The Art of War* does not directly discuss procurement. Nevertheless, it's specifically mentioned that we should enter into alliances with others only when we are acquainted with their designs. This idea relates to business in that, for a project's success, a vendor has to be chosen based on the needs of the project, and the decision should be based on the strategic needs of the organization in that the vendor should help in achieving long-term goals. An argument along similar lines about vendor selection can also be found in PMBOK®.

In the following chapters, the similarities with knowledge areas in PMBOK® and processes within the knowledge areas are further discussed and are analyzed in brief. Chapter titles from chapter four to chapter twelve are similar to what knowledge areas are known as.

CHAPTER 2

The General

Alexander the Great, Hannibal, Asoka, Napoleon, and the list go on—it doesn't take much knowledge of history to agree that history is full of tales of generals who have led thousands. Some of them conquered the world, and the others were known for their strategic and tactical skills on the battleground.

Most of us must have heard the names that are mentioned above. All these men are some of the most famous generals in the history of the world. They had armies and thousands of soldiers at their command. They conquered lands, were victorious against the strongest, expanded their kingdoms, and in turn established rule over millions. Expansion of the kingdoms was one of the only ways of establishing supremacy in the times they walked this earth. These men were equipped with modern artillery, they had armies of skilled professional soldiers, and they were master strategists and tacticians. These men are known for how well they conducted the wars. The men led several battles with thousands of soldiers and several hundred types of weapons. There were times when the task at hand was deadly. Sometimes their existence was threatened, and in the other times, it was an easy, straightforward planned act of war. Sun Tzu wrote his book for such generals with the purpose of giving them a methodology for conducting war. In addition to the methodology, this book states many times the qualities that a general needs to have to ensure victory in war. Replace the term *general* from the situation above with *project manager*, and, given that a project is about achieving positive outcomes amid conflicting needs and interests and perhaps lead to the rise and fall of stakeholders, the leadership qualities that Sun Tzu states that a general should have are also needed in a project manager.

About the general, Sun Tzu says, *"Now the general is the bulwark of the state; if the bulwark is complete at all points; the state will be strong; if the bulwark is defective, the state will be weak."*

The role of a project manager varies from a facilitator—one who has to ensure that all elements contributing to success come together to push the project toward success—to a warrior, a dramatic term that signifies the situation to which a project manager is often exposed. While a facilitator is someone who makes sure all the activities are coordinated in a project, the warrior has to ensure the battlefield is set in such a way that the result is the victory.

A project manager is a corporate world general.

A project manager must understand *self*. The self can be thought of the collective of organizational capabilities and interpersonal skills. A project manager should also possess an understanding of the challenge. The project strategy should be driven based on this understanding that keeps improving as one moves forward in the project drives decisions, outcomes, and the success of the project.

In this chapter, you will read statements from *The Art of War* and how they apply to project managers. The quotations from *The Art of War* are in arrow symbols. These statements about generals can be applied to conduct, the qualities, the personality, and actions of a project manager who is destined to be victorious. While some of them are focused on personal traits, there are other statements that can be thought of as referring to a project manager's knowledge about application areas (challenges), organizational culture, understanding of decision making in stakeholders' interests, skill assessment as per the needs of the project, and understanding of the project dependencies.

The quotations from *The Art of War* come first, followed by their application in project management in *italics*.

In the Chapter, **LAYING PLANS** of *The Art of War* Sun Tzu discusses the traits and qualification of a commander, in the following quotations.

→ The *commander* stands for the virtues of wisdom, sincerity, benevolence, courage, and strictness.

> *In our times, it is interpreted as 'A good leader should be wise (in making decisions), trustworthy (should inspire trust), caring (taking care of the team), courageous (to make tough choices), and strict (in ensuring compliance). To be effective, a project manager must possess a balance of technical, interpersonal, and conceptual skills that help him to analyze situations and act appropriately. Some of the important interpersonal skills to have include leadership, team building, motivation, communication, influence, the ability to make decisions, political and cultural awareness, and negotiation.'*

→ *The Art of War*, then, is governed by five constant factors to be taken into account in one's deliberations when seeking to determine the conditions in the field.

→ These are (1) The moral Law; (2) Heaven; (3) Earth; (4) the commander; (5) method and discipline.

> *These statements lead you to the meaning that 'A project manager should be familiar with organizational culture*

> *and norms, enterprise environmental factors, organizational process assets, and organizational structure. He should also possess good leadership and interpersonal skills. A project manager who possesses all these skills and knowledge will be a successful project manager.'*

→ Now the general who wins a battle makes many calculations in his temple before the battle is fought.

> *This means that an 'Effective project managers have good decision-making skills. To be effective, it is important to rate the pros and cons of alternatives, select the best solution, create action plans for proper solutions, and evaluate all possible solutions before deciding on one. A project manager who spends time in planning the solution before embarking on the project has a much greater chance of success.'*

Chapter, **WAGING WAR** has some more quotes about the general of the Army.

→ Thus, it may be known that the leader of armies is the arbiter of the people's fate, the man on whom it depends whether the nation shall be in peace or in peril.

> *This quotation comments on the desirable qualities a project manager should possess and carries a meaning that 'Project success and failure depends on the leadership qualities of the project manager. These qualities could have an impact on the future of the organization he is part of and also on the future of other team members in the project/organization.'*

→ Therefore, the skilful leader subdues the enemy's troops without any fighting; he captures their cities without laying siege to them; he overthrows their kingdom without lengthy operations in the field.

→ With his forces intact, he will dispute the mastery of the empire, and thus, without losing a man, his triumph will be complete. This is the method of attacking by stratagem.

> *The statements clearly indicate that 'A skilled project manager is able to achieve project success and avert failures using his knowledge and skills effectively. A combination of great leadership, decision-making and negotiation skills along with the skilful use of politics and power will ensure that project risks are curtailed, and chances of project success improved to a great extent.'*

→ Now the general is the bulwark of the state; if the bulwark is complete at all points, the state will be strong; if the bulwark is defective, the state will be weak.

> *This is a powerful idea from Sun Tzu, which indicates, 'An organization is as good as its leadership team, or a project is as good as its project manager. If the project manager is weak, then the project is more likely to be seen as a failure. Likewise, an organization with a weak leadership team will be a weak organization.'*

→ There are three ways in which a ruler can bring misfortune upon his army:

  → (1) By commanding the army to advance or to retreat, being ignorant of the fact that it cannot obey. This is called hobbling the army.

  → (2) By attempting to govern an army in the same way as he administers a kingdom, being ignorant of the conditions which obtain in an army. This causes restlessness in the soldiers' minds.

  → (3) By employing the officers of his army without discrimination, through ignorance of the military principle of adaptation to circumstances. This shakes the confidence of the soldiers."

Leadership qualities of the general are a repeated theme in *The Art of War*. '*A project manager requires strong leadership skills for creating high-performance teams. It is important to communicate the vision and inspire the team toward the common goal. The project manager should take into consideration the organizational structure, team dynamics, and other environmental factors while building and managing the team. Team building can be further enhanced by introducing appropriate rewards, by employing recognition and ethics, by managing conflicts effectively, by promoting trust and open communication among team members, and by providing strong leadership. Project managers must clearly articulate policies and procedures and lead by example by following them. A lack of these skills could lead to decreased team morale, low performing teams, and potential failure of the project.*'

→ Thus, we may know that there are five essentials for victory:

- → (1) He will win who knows when to fight and when not to fight.
- → (2) He will win who knows how to handle both superior and inferior forces.
- → (3) He will win whose army is animated by the same spirit throughout all its ranks.
- → (4) He will win who, prepared himself, waits to take the enemy unprepared.
- → (5) He will win who has military capacity and is not interfered with by the sovereign.

'A successful project manager will have good influencing skills and will know how to handle all the stakeholders in the project. He has the skills to make the right decisions and to influence and motivate the entire project team. He creates and nurtures high performing teams. The skillful use of power and politics and the ability to negotiate and influence helps him to be successful.'

→ If you know the enemy and know yourself, you need not fear the result of a hundred battles. If you know yourself but not the enemy, for every victory gained you will also suffer a defeat. If you know neither the enemy nor yourself, you will succumb in every battle.

'To be successful in projects, it is important to be aware of politics and how to handle it. A good project manager must know his supporters and opponents within the organization. He should be aware of internal and external politics and

> *other such factors that may alter the project's performance. Knowing how to deal with politics gives you a better chance of success. Your chances of success are diminished if you are not able to handle politics rightly.'*

About the general of the Army, in Chapter **TACTICAL DISPOSITIONS** of The Art of War, Sun Tzu observes the following. These quotations highlights the analytical abilities of the project manager.

→ The good fighters of old first put themselves beyond the possibility of defeat and then waited for an opportunity for defeating the enemy.

→ To secure ourselves against defeat lies in our own hands, but the opportunity of defeating the enemy is provided by the enemy himself.

→ Thus, the good fighter is able to secure himself against defeat but cannot make certain of defeating the enemy.

> 'Effective project managers use their technical, conceptual, and interpersonal skills to analyze all potential situations and risks with the project and plan to avoid project failure. The primary message is that, a project manager must be able to minimize the probability of potential project failure before he starts to analyze and evaluate options to enhance project success'.

→ What the ancients called a clever fighter is one who not only wins, but excels in winning with ease.

→ Hence his victories bring him neither reputation for wisdom nor credit for courage.

> 'A skilled project manager is not only one who ensures project success, but also delivers the projects within the expectations set on time, cost, and quality. The second line is a testimony to the fact that project managers who constantly deliver projects within set expectations rarely get credit in the industry or make the news.'

→ The consummate leader cultivates the moral law, and strictly adheres to method and discipline; thus it is in his power to control success.

> 'A skilled project manager promotes organizational culture, values, and norms and strictly adheres to the standards and processes defined in the organizational process assets. The project managers enhance their abilities to create highly effective teams by promoting the values, norms, and processes to the entire team, thereby ensure greater chances of project's success.'

Sun Tzu, in the chapter about **ENERGY**, says the following how a general should conduct war, to ensure victory.

→ Therefore, the good fighter will be terrible in his onset and prompt in his decision.

> 'A skilled project manager will have excellent decision-making skills.'

The Comparison

→ The clever combatant looks to the effect of combined energy and does not require too much from individuals.

→ When he utilizes combined energy, his fighting men become as it were like unto rolling logs or stones. For it is the nature of a log or stone to remain motionless on level ground and to move when on a slope; if four-cornered, to come to a standstill, but if round-shaped, to go rolling down.

> 'A skilled project manager puts the team above individuals. He understands and recognizes the importance of teamwork and develops an environment that fosters and promotes teamwork.'

In the chapter titled **WEAK POINTS AND STRONG POINTS** Sun Tzu states that

→ All men can see the tactics whereby I conquer, but what none can see is the strategy out of which victory is evolved.

> Which clearly means, 'What everyone sees is the tactical methods adopted by the project manager during the execution of the project. What they do not see is the long period of planning and strategizing that preceded the project.'

→ He who can modify his tactics in relation to his opponent and thereby succeed in winning may be called a heaven-born captain.

> 'An effective project manager needs to be flexible with his tactics and be able to modify his tactics based on the current circumstances and environmental factors.'

About the general, Sun Tzu says, in **MANEUVERING**;

→ A clever general, therefore, avoids an army when its spirit is keen, but attacks it when it is sluggish and inclined to return. This is the art of studying moods.

> 'A skilled project manager ensures that the actions are timely for the benefit of the project.'

The chapter **VARIATION IN TACTICS** takes a note about how an insightful general can lead the state to victory.

→ The general who thoroughly understands the advantages that accompany variation of tactics knows how to handle his troops.

→ The general who does not understand these may be well acquainted with the configuration of the country, yet he will not be able to turn his knowledge to practical account.

> In the modern world context, it means that 'A skilled project manager will be flexible with tactics and the handling of his team. It is important to be flexible to be able to improve the chances of project success.'

- There are five dangerous faults which may affect a general:
  - (1) Recklessness, which leads to destruction
  - (2) Cowardice, which leads to capture
  - (3) A hasty temper, which can be provoked by insults
  - (4) A delicacy of honor which is sensitive to shame
  - (5) Over-solicitude for his men, which exposes him to worry and trouble
- These are the five besetting sins of a general, ruinous to the conduct of war.

These are very relevant aspects of project manager's personal traits; '(1) Recklessness can be thought of as hasty decision-making without adequate planning and/or not following proper risk management practices. (2) Cowardice could be construed as the inability to make the right but difficult decisions that one may often need to take during the course of a project. (3) A hasty temper can be thought of as having improper communication and/or a lack of political or cultural awareness in dealing with stakeholders. (4) Sensitivity to shame could refer to his interpersonal skills and might make him second guess his decisions too often for fear of failure. (5) A good leader may have to make difficult decisions that may be against the short-term interests of his team. All of the above qualities can potentially lead to bad project performance.'

In the chapter, **THE ARMY ON THE MARCH**, Sun Tzu has insisted that a general must treat his men well and with respect and it's an obvious fact that a project manager, who shows disrespect to his team, doesn't succeed in the end.

→ If a general shows confidence in his men but always insists on his orders being obeyed, the gain will be mutual.

> *'A good project manager should be an effective leader, as well. He should show confidence in his team and help the team to grow. A skilled project manager would know how to wield his various powers—expert power, formal power, coercive power, referent power and reward power—to the right degree to extract the best from his team.'*

The chapter **TERRAIN**, in *The Art of War* quotes Sun Tzu says;

→ The general who advances without coveting fame and retreats without fearing disgrace, whose only thought is to protect his country and do good service for his sovereign, is the jewel of the kingdom.

> This quotation carries the message of focus and being objective. *'A project manager is only bothered about the success of the project and the organization. He would prefer to close a project that is destined for failure and save the organization than worry about the disgrace in being associated with a failed project.'*

→ Regard your soldiers as your children and they will follow you into the deepest valleys; look upon them as your own beloved sons, and they will stand by you even unto death.

> The statement above reiterates that *the team should be respected. Earn the respect and trust of your team and*

> the members will do anything for you. Respect and trust, rather than fear and submission, are the key elements of effective leadership.

THE NINE SITUATIONS, a chapter in *The Art of War* mentions following about the army men;

→ Carefully study the well-being of your men and do not overtax them. Concentrate your energy, and hoard your strength. Keep your army continually on the move and devise unfathomable plans.

→ Throw your soldiers into positions whence there is no escape, and they will prefer death to flight. If they will face death, there is nothing they may not achieve. Officers and men alike will put forth their uttermost strength.

> In the world of project management, it obviously is about task assignments and skill utilization of the team. 'A leader should look after the well being of his team. Invest in building your team. Give them challenging problems to bring the best out of the team.'

In the chapter, **THE ATTACK BY FIRE**, Sun Tzu states that the King is as important in the success of a general in any campaign.

→ The enlightened ruler lays his plans well ahead; the good general cultivates his resources.

> This interprets as, 'A skilled project manager invests in his team and keeps them motivated. He introduces

> *appropriate rewards and recognition, thereby eliciting the team members' commitment to him and the projects. The sponsor, on the other hand, works with foresight and ensures the project manager gets the required support to succeed.'*

In an aptly titled chapter **THE USE OF SPIES**, Sun Tzu reiterates on the importance gathering intelligence.

→ It is only the enlightened ruler and the wise general who will use the highest intelligence of the army for purposes of spying and thereby they achieve great results. Spies are a most important element in water because on them depends an army's ability to move.

> In the corporate world, this means that *'both the project sponsor and the project manager should devise mechanisms to continue to gather information. The skilled project sponsor and project manager with the right knowledge and wisdom understand the importance of information gathering. With right decision-making skills, they use this information to achieve greater results.'*

In the next chapter, we will have a look at Sun Tzu's ideas and statements about the Enterprise environmental factors in his timeless classic, *The Art of War*.

CHAPTER 3

The Environment

Like any other endeavor, a project outcome is also deeply impacted by the environment in which it is executed. Therefore, one has to keep the project environment in mind while designing, strategizing, planning, and making any decisions about the project. These influencing factors can be related to the internal or external environment of the performing organizations. They can be from within or outside of the performing organization. These factors can potentially impact the organization positively or negatively. Many such factors, either directly or indirectly, become risks, issues, and constraints of a project. Some of the prominent examples of these factors are organizational culture, the organization's structure, processes, marketplace conditions, regulatory and quality standards related to the business, national, regional and global political climate, availability of skilled human resources in the organization and in the market, and the organization's policies related to customers, people, projects, and project management.

Sun Tzu also discussed the environments in which the general operates and stated that it has a direct impact on the victory in war.

This chapter discusses the ideas from *The Art of War* concerning the environmental influencing factors and their relevance to a project manager.

In the chapter, **LAYING PLANS**, Sun Tzu says that

→ The Moral Law causes the people to be in complete accord with their ruler so that they will follow him regardless of their lives, undismayed by any danger.

> When interpreted, it means that, *'The organizations tend to develop cultures unique to them and manifest in numerous ways, such as shared vision, values, norms, beliefs and expectations, policies, methods and procedures, relationships with authority, and work ethics. The organizational culture and norms ensure that the project team follows authority and works toward the vision.'*

→ By method and discipline are to be understood the marshaling of the army in its proper subdivisions, the graduations of rank among the officers, the maintenance of roads by which supplies may reach the army, and the control of military expenditure.

> I interpret it as, *'Organizational structure is an influencing factor in executing the projects. The reference here is to a classical functional organization with hierarchically grouped teams. A project manager should be aware of the organizational structure, and should know how to manage the team within the given organizational structure, however, constrained it may be.'*

→ By means of these seven considerations, I can forecast victory or defeat:

The Comparison

→ (1) Which of the two sovereigns is imbued with the Moral Law?

→ (2) Which of the two generals has most ability?

→ (3) With whom lie the advantages derived from Heaven and Earth?

→ (4) On which side is discipline most rigorously enforced?

→ (5) Which army is stronger?

→ (6) On which side are officers and men more highly trained?

→ (7) In which army is there the greater constancy both in reward and punishment?

> Sun Tzu has emphasized on the criticality of the factors related to measures like discipline, skills, rewards and punishment in his book, for project manager, it means that, *'An organization with a strong culture and norms has a greater chance of succeeding in projects. Other factors that increase the chances of project success are standardized guidelines, work instructions, and having organizational standards and policies (e.g., training, rewards and recognition, and performance measurement criteria). A good leadership team is also an important factor in improving the organization's chances of succeeding in projects.'*

Some more similarities about Enterprise Environmental Factors are found in the chapter titled **ENERGY**:

→ The control of a large force is the same principle as the control of a few men: it is merely a question of dividing up their numbers.

→ Fighting with a large army under your command is no wise different from fighting with a small one: it is merely a question of instituting signs and signals.

Organizational structure is an influencing factor in how projects can be run. The project manager must understand the organizational structures and choose the appropriate method of managing the team. Different structures require that you approach them differently and institute different processes and procedures to govern the project. Projects of all sizes and magnitudes can be managed with ease provided smaller teams are created and appropriate processes, tools and communication mechanisms are deployed.

→ In all fighting, the direct method may be used for joining battle, but indirect methods will be needed in order to secure victory.

→ Indirect tactics, efficiently applied, are inexhaustible as Heaven and Earth, unending as the flow of rivers and streams; like the sun and moon, they end but to begin anew; like the four seasons, they pass away to return once more.

Though the project must be executed as per plan, it is the flawless inclusion of the unplanned activities into the plan that pushes projects towards a successful outcome. These unplanned activities, tasks will arise as the project progresses and such tasks must be acted upon as they impact a project's success positively.

Sun Tzu, in the chapter, **VARIATION IN TACTICS**, says that;

→ In war, the general receives his commands from the sovereign, collects his army, and concentrates his forces.

> This indicates that, *'There are many types of organizational structures. The project manager is appointed by the project sponsor and receives instructions from the sponsor. Based on the organization structure, (functional, matrix, or projected), he has varying degrees of authority and control over the team. Nevertheless, the project manager must be appointed and only then a plan can be put in place, and the team can be assembled.'*

Sun Tzu, in chapter **TERRAIN**, says the following about the influence of the environment;

→ When the common soldiers are too strong and their officers too weak, the result is insubordination.

→ When the officers are too strong and the common soldiers too weak, the result is collapse.

→ When the higher officers are angry and insubordinate, and on meeting the enemy give battle on their own account from a feeling of resentment, before the commander-in-chief can tell whether or no he is in a position to fight, the result is ruin.

> To a project manager it means that, *'The organizational structure and the calibre of the leadership team have an impact on the performance of the team. A relatively stronger team with a relatively weak leadership would result in fierce resentment among the team and insubordination. If the leadership is too strong and the team is very weak, it will lead to collapse of the team. Having an insubordinate team will lead to ruin.'*

→ When the general is weak and without authority; when his orders are not clear and distinct; when there are no fixed duties assigned to officers and men, and the ranks are formed in a slovenly, haphazard manner, the result is utter disorganization.

→ When a general, unable to estimate the enemy's strength, allows an inferior force to engage a larger one, or hurls a weak detachment against a powerful one and neglects to place picked soldiers in the front rank, the result must be rout.

> These quotes from *The Art of War*, highlight that, 'Having a project manager without proper authority and leadership skills will result in utter disorganization. There will be no defined roles and responsibilities for team members, and the team would be chosen in a haphazard manner, resulting in chaos. When the project manager lacks technical and leadership skills, he will commit grave mistakes, leading to project failures.'

Next, in chapter 4 to chapter 12, we will explore Sun Tzu's message for the project manager in the context of each knowledge area described in PMBOK®.

Reader's Notes

CHAPTER 4

Project Integration Management

Project Integration management is about an integrated approach to the complete project. This must take into account all the management activities involved in all phases of a project through its life cycle. So the activities must start with the initiation phase that is defined by the project charter. Other major processes involved in the overall process are developing the project management plan, managing project execution, monitoring and controlling of project work, and closing of the project or a phase.

As they say, change is the only constant, and it happens throughout the lifetime of a project. That's a reality for any project. Managing these changes and integrating the approved changes to the project are crucial activities for ensuring project success. The project Integration knowledge area has set of processes and activities that are needed to identify, define, combine, unify, and coordinate the various processes and project management activities to integrate all these processes and help to manage the interacting and iterative processes well.

The overall integration management process is actually a collection of five distinct processes that have an impact, influence each other, and are related to specific phases of the project management life cycle. The sequence starts with the project charter development that defines the start of the project. The development of the project management plan relates to all the phases in the project life cycle. The process in 'direct and manage project execution' and 'monitor and control project' work together to define how the ongoing work will be managed and monitored. Closing of the project or the current phase is about managing the project or phase closure. During all these phases, the integrated change management plan is the tool to manage changes systematically. Being so interlinked, any changes in one have consequential changes in the other processes. These changes need to be tracked, and the project manager must very carefully take care of all these linked issues.

> *The Art of War emphasizes a concept similar to the project charter: the sovereign selects a general with all the necessary qualities; good fighting skills, the ability to handle superior and inferior forces, etc.; Then trusts him to win the war without any interference from the sovereign. There is a lot of emphasis on the development of a good plan or strategy prior to entering the battle.* The Art of War *emphasizes that a general must ensure proper execution of plans and continue to review progress to pick up any indication that suggests modifications to the current strategy/plan.*

In the following sections, let's see how Sun Tzu's *The Art of War* is similar to the processes in project Integration Management knowledge area of PMBOK®.

4.1 Develop Project Charter

A project charter formally authorizes the start of a project, authorizes the project manager (PM) to assign resources to the project, documents the business needs and justification, describes the customer's requirements, and links the project to the ongoing work of the organization. The charter officially sanctions the project. Without a charter, the project cannot begin. During multiphase projects, the PM validates the decisions made during the original chartering of the project. The project charter also authorizes the next charter phase and updates the existing charter.

In the chapter **ATTACK BY STRATAGEM** we find following statements about the victory in war;

→ Thus, we may know that there are five essentials for victory:

→ (1) He will win who knows when to fight and when not to fight.

→ (2) He will win who knows how to handle both superior and inferior forces.

→ (3) He will win whose army is animated by the same spirit throughout all its ranks.

→ (4) He will win who, prepared himself, waits to take the enemy unprepared.

→ (5) He will win who has military capacity and is not interfered with by the sovereign.

> Just like for the victory in wars, 'For the success of a project, it is important that the project manager is accepted by all stakeholders—the ones he reports to and the ones who report to him. The project sponsor should select the right person for the job and then give him the freedom to get the job done without any interference. It is the sponsor's function to give broad instructions, but decisions regarding the project should be left to the project manager. A project charter is akin to the marching orders of an army general.'

4.2 Develop Project Management Plan

The purpose of this process is to produce an integrated project management plan that defines how the project is executed, monitored, and controlled, and that describes the processes to follow while performing each phase of the project. This is the first process in the planning group and should be performed first.

Chapter **LAYING PLANS**, Sun Tzu observes;

→ It is a matter of life and death, a road either to safety or to ruin. Hence it is a subject of inquiry which can on no account be neglected.

> *'Developing a well-thought-out and detailed project plan is essential and decides the outcome (success or failure) of a project.'*

→ Now the general who wins a battle makes many calculations in his temple before the battle is fought.

> *'Carefully elaborate on the project plan before starting the project, until you are comfortable with the plan. A project's success or failure depends on the level of planning.'*

In Chapter **TACTICAL DISPOSITIONS**, there is another quote about planning;

→ Thus, it is that in war, the victorious strategist only seeks battle after the victory has been won, whereas he who is destined to defeat first fights and afterwards looks for victory.

Project Integration Management

> *'First lay plans that will ensure project success, and then embark on the project. Relying on execution alone without planning will not ensure project success.'*

4.3 Direct and Manage Project Execution

The activities in this process are expected to help in accomplishing the project objectives, goals and success criteria, to help implement the planned methods and standards, help create control, verify and validate project deliverables, and to select and manage sellers. A project plan serves as a baseline. A project manager should continually compare and monitor project performance against the baseline so that corrective action may be taken.

Sun Tzu, in the chapter, **LAYING PLANS**, says;

→ One should modify one's plans according to the favorability of circumstances.

> *'Planning is an ongoing process. The project plan should be monitored constantly and refined depending on changing circumstances during the course of the project.'*

In chapter, **TACTICAL DISPOSITIONS**, he observes;

→ Hence the skillful fighter puts himself into a position that makes defeat impossible and does not miss the moment for defeating the enemy.

> *'A skillful project manager will direct and manage all arrangements and preparations to ensure the project does*

> *not fail. By careful planning, he also increases the chances of project success.'*

And in chapter **WEAK POINTS AND STRONG POINTS**, Sun Tzu reiterates the importance of planning and observes;

→ Whoever is first in the field and awaits the coming of the enemy will be fresh for the fight; whoever is second in the field and has to hasten to battle will arrive exhausted.

'Plan the work, and then work the plan. A skillful project manager will plan ahead and prepare beforehand to deal with all potential risks. He then stays on top of the execution of this plan.'

4.4 Monitor and Control Project Work

This process helps in reviewing, tracking, and controlling project progress. It ensures that the performance objectives outlined in the project management plan are met. Monitoring and measuring project performance by comparing it with the established project baseline helps to identify variances and get the project back on track. The analysis of performance data helps to determine whether corrective or preventive actions are needed to control the project performance.

Chapter **TACTICAL DISPOSITIONS**, *The Art of War* quotes;

→ He wins his battles by making no mistakes. Making no mistakes is what establishes the certainty of victory, for it means conquering an enemy that is already defeated.

> *'The project work should be monitored, to ensure work is proceeding according to plan. Making no mistakes establishes the certainty of project success.'*

Sun Tzu, in chapter **WEAK POINTS AND STRONG POINTS**, observes that

- → Appear at points which the enemy must hasten to defend; march swiftly to places where you are not expected.

  > This means, *'Monitor the plans, measure progress, and make dynamic changes to the plans based on progress measures and new realities on the ground.'*

- → You can be sure of succeeding in your attacks if you attack only places that are undefended.

  > In a project management world, *'Monitoring the changing environmental factors, updating the plan and acting on these changes ensure success. Monitoring and controlling execution of plans gives you the best opportunity to succeed.'*

Interestingly, in the chapter, **THE ATTACK BY FIRE**, I found some quotes that are relevant to the project managers;

- → In attacking with fire, one should be prepared to meet five possible developments:
- → When fire breaks out inside the enemy's camp, respond at once with an attack from without.
- → If there is an outbreak of fire, but the enemy's soldiers remain quiet, bide your time and do not attack.
- → When the force of the flames has reached its height, follow

- → it up with an attack, if that is practicable; if not, stay where you are.
- → If it is possible to make an assault with fire from without, do not wait for it to break out within, but deliver your attack at a favorable moment.
- → When you start a fire, be to windward of it. Do not attack from the leeward.

The above mentioned statements can be interpreted as, 'Compare actual performance against the project management plan and look for variances. Assess performance to determine if any corrective or preventive actions are needed, and then take those steps as necessary. Identify new risks and monitor existing project risks to make sure the risks are identified and appropriate risk responses are being executed.'

- → In every army, the five developments connected with fire must be known, the movements of the stars calculated, and a watch kept for the proper days.

'Analyze, track, and monitor existing project risks to make sure the risks are identified and appropriate risk responses are being executed.'

4.6 Perform Integrated Change Control

A project manager may have to deal with budget cuts and subsequently the project may have to be re-planned. This process helps a project manager to deal with such a situation. Perform Integrated Change Control process is about maintaining the performance baselines within acceptable limits. The purpose is to review all change requests, approve and control changes to the deliverables while focusing on the influencing factors that cause changes, managing approved changes maintaining the integrity of the project baselines and reviewing and analyzing preventive and corrective actions.

In chapter, **WEAK POINTS AND STRONG POINTS**, Sun Tzu says;

→ Therefore, just as water retains no constant shape, so in warfare there are no constant conditions.

> 'Anticipate changes and make plans to accommodate these changes'.

→ He who can modify his tactics in relation to his opponent and thereby succeed in winning may be called a heaven-born captain.

> *This is a very practical profound statement, 'The project manager should keep the plan flexible and hence should always be ready to analyze changes are per change management process. Monitor changes and make necessary changes to the baseline plan to ensure project success.'*

4.7 Close Project or Phase

The process of closing a project or phase involves gathering project records and disseminating information to formalize the acceptance of the product, service, or result. Analyze the project management process to determine the effectiveness, and document the lessons learned.

> *Though there isn't any direct reference to the disbanding of an army,* The Art of War *does emphasize making use of experiences and learning picked up during wars and battles, e.g. movements and placement of troops, knowledge and understanding of heaven and earth, etc. (section 5.2)*

In the next chapter, we will explore *The Art of War* from the perspective of managing the scope of the project.

Reader's Notes

CHAPTER 5

Project Scope Management

Doing the work required for completion of your project is essential for the success of your project. Similarly, if something that is not required for the project is to be done, it will be a wasted effort. It adds to the cost and the timeline of the project. Therefore, it is essential that exactly what needs to be done and what is not included in the requirements be very clearly identified. The process in the Scope Management knowledge area helps in this regard.

In the scope management situation, the scope refers to either a product scope and/or a project scope. A *product scope* refers to the details of a product, its features, and functionalities or it refers to a service or result. A *project scope* refers to work required to deliver that product, service, or result. To manage the project scope, it is necessary to manage several contributing processes that help a PM complete scope management-related activities. These include collecting requirements, defining scope, creating a work breakdown structure, verifying scope, and controlling scope. These activities will have to be undertaken at least once during the life cycle of the project.

Collecting requirements involves articulating and documenting the requirements. Stakeholders have to be involved, and eliciting requirements from them is a vital activity. This is the phase that determines what exactly needs to be done and what need not be undertaken. Defining the scope involves detailing the requirements. The WBS defines more detailed steps or tasks to be undertaken to achieve each of the requirements that were developed earlier.

Verifying scope is essential to make sure the requirements capture the necessary goals of the project and/or the product and there are no unrealistic needs stated. The requirements can change. There are several ways additional requirements can creep into the project scope unless controlled properly. It may be due to some need that was not understood clearly, and extra work is indicated later. It is also possible that an entirely new requirement comes up. The customer may simply demand a new feature. Changed market conditions necessitate an entirely new feature or implementation of an existing feature in a new way. Whatever it is, it is practical to realize that some changes will take place. What is required is control over the changes so that your project does not run away in terms of cost and time budget.

A project scope statement, the WBS, and a WBS dictionary define the project scope baseline. The scope management and the control plan refer to this baseline in an ongoing manner.

There is obviously some planning required for carrying out the necessary activities of the scope management plan. This planning is part of the project management plan development. The scope management plan generated out of this activity would guide the scope definition, documentation, verification, management, and control. The actual documentation produced is guided by the standards prevalent in the organization as well as the "needs" of the project. These will determine how detailed the documentation will be and how formal or informal it is going to be.

Project charter and stakeholder-related information are critical to this process. Various methods and means such as interviews, focus-groups, workshops, group creativity, decision-making techniques, questionnaires, product analysis, alternatives identification, organizational process assets, and surveys, as well as, observations and the development of a prototype are used to form a scope baseline, scope verification mechanisms, and scope management plan.

> *The Art of War talks about ensuring adequate resources and being prepared before going into battle. It talks about measurements, estimations, and calculations for improving chances of victory. These are similar to the steps involved in creating a good WBS. There is also adequate reference to verifying and controlling the scope, similar to PMBOK®.*

Lets see how each process in the project Scope Management knowledge area has similarity with *The Art of War*.

5.1 Collect Requirements

This process helps a project manager to define and document stakeholders' needs to meet the project objectives. Information about requirements is elicited from stakeholders and documented in requirements documentation. The document requirements reflect the project objectives and have a direct relationship with the project's outcome.

In the chapter, **THE USE OF SPIES**;

→ The Art of War recognizes nine varieties of ground: (1) dispersive ground, (2) facile ground, (3) contentious ground, (4) open ground, (5) ground of intersecting highways, (6) serious ground, (7) difficult ground, (8) hemmed-in ground, (9) desperate ground.

In chapter, **TERRAIN**, Sun Tzu states the following;

→ If we know that the enemy is open to attack and also know that our men are in a condition to attack, but are unaware that the nature of the ground makes fighting impracticable, we have still gone only halfway towards victory.

And in the chapter, **THE NINE SITUATIONS**, I came across a statement about understanding the requirements,

→ Success in warfare is gained by carefully accommodating ourselves to the enemy's purpose.

> 'There are many statements in The Art of War that mandate that a general identify the requirements to win the battle. As a matter of fact, almost the entire book is dedicated to this aspect. Sun Tzu commands a general to gather information about the battleground, to consider his own and the enemy's readiness for the battle, and to be flexible about the goals.'

5.2 Define Scope

A detailed description of the project and the product is developed during the scope definition. The process helps in creating a detailed project scope statement. It's critical to the project success and builds upon the deliverables, assumptions, and constraints established during project initiation. During planning, the project scope is defined and described with greater specificity as more information about the project is known. Let's have a quick look at Sun Tzu's views about scope definition.

In the chapter, **THE USE OF SPIES**, Sun Tzu makes says that,

→ Thus, what enables the wise sovereign and the good general to strike and conquer, and achieve things beyond the reach of ordinary men, is foreknowledge.

> *'The project manager and senior stakeholders must keep themselves informed necessary information about the project. It is also important to have information on the potential risks in a project. Having such information beforehand ensures the chances of project success.'*

→ Now this foreknowledge cannot be elicited from spirits; it cannot be obtained inductively from experience, nor by any deductive calculation.

→ Knowledge of the enemy's dispositions can be obtained only from other men.

→ Hence the use of spies, of whom there are five classes, (1) local spies, (2) inward spies, (3) converted spies, (4) doomed spies, and (5) surviving spies.

> The quotes above indicate that, *'In some cases, information about all potential risks cannot be obtained from prior experience (lessons learned) or from deductive calculation. This information can be obtained only through skilled experts or subject matter experts.'*

→ Spies cannot be usefully employed without a certain intuitive sagacity.

→ Without subtle ingenuity of mind, one cannot make certain of the truth of their reports.

> This, to a project manager, means that, *'Employ proper means to distill the information received from the experts. Use proper methods to analyze the information, find alternatives, and make decisions.'*

5.3 Create WBS

This process helps in subdividing the major project deliverables and project work into smaller, more manageable components. A WBS defines the scope of the project and organizes the project into deliverable-oriented, hierarchically decomposed work assigned to the project team. A WBS always represents the current approved scope statement. We will now go to references that are similar to creating a WBS in *The Art of War*.

Chapter titled, **TACTICAL DISPOSITIONS** contains a powerful idea;

→ Hence the skillful fighter puts himself into a position that makes defeat impossible and does not miss the moment for defeating the enemy.

> This is an all encompassing statement. *'Essentially means that the project manager must take into account all the major project deliverables, that would lead to the desired project outcome, effectively saying that a WBS must be created with the complete scope of the project.'*

In the chapter, **WAGING WAR**, we come across following statements,

→ The skillful soldier does not raise a second levy, neither are his supply wagons loaded more than twice.

The Comparison

→ Bring war material with you from home, but forage on the enemy. Thus, the army will have food enough for its needs.

> In the corporate world, it translates as, '*A skillful project manager will ensure adequate resources are planned, and necessary resources are secured on time, when the project needs them. While creating the WBS, he would also estimate the type and quantity of resources required and secures the resources.*'

Chapter **TACTICAL DISPOSITIONS**, has the following two statements;

→ In respect of military method, we have, firstly, Measurement; secondly, Estimation of quantity; thirdly, Calculation; fourthly, Balancing of chances; fifthly, Victory.

→ Measurement owes its existence to Earth; Estimation of quantity to Measurement; Calculation to Estimation of quantity; Balancing of chances to Calculation; and Victory to Balancing of chances.

> The number crunching isn't modern after all! 'Measurements, estimations, calculations, and balancing of chances are all important for achieving project success. Interestingly, these steps are also involved in creating a WBS.'

5.4 Verify Scope

The purpose of this process is to obtain the stakeholders' formal acceptance of the completed project deliverables and obtain a sign-off stating that the deliverables are satisfactory and meet stakeholders' expectations.

Sun Tzu, in the chapter, **VARIATIONS IN TACTICS**, observes that;

→ The Art of War teaches us to rely, not on the likelihood of the enemy's not coming, but on our own readiness to receive him; not on the chance of his not attacking, but rather on the fact that we have made our position unassailable.

> It can be interpreted that, *'Scope verification helps in ensuring the solutions delivered are consistent with the desired project outcome. This means that the organization's positions are satisfactory and unassailable.'*

5.5 Control Scope

This process helps to monitor the status of the scope and manage changes to the scope baseline. It ensures all requested changes and recommended corrective or preventive actions are processed through the project integrated change control process. Work results must be monitored to ensure that they match expected outcomes. This process helps in managing the actual changes when they occur and in ensuring that the changes are integrated with the other control processes. Most importantly, they help in avoiding scope creep, the zero-dollar change requests. Let's see what Sun Tzu says about controlling the project scope.

The Comparison

The chapter **MANEUVERING**, in *The Art of War* quotes;

→ After that, comes tactical maneuvering, than which there is nothing more difficult. The difficulty of tactical maneuvering consists of turning the devious into the direct and misfortune into gain.

> It must be acknowledged that *'Changes may occur to the original plans once the project commences. Therefore, it is needed to manage changes to the project baselines in such a way that the project outcome is achieved.'*

→ Maneuvering with an army is advantageous; with an undisciplined multitude, most dangerous.

> With this we can interpret, *'Changes can only be successfully managed and integrated with the project when we have a change management process defined to control the project scope. This statement also hints at the importance and need for monitoring and controlling the laid-out plans (WBS).*

→ Whether to concentrate or to divide your troops must be decided by circumstances.

> This is about decision making. *'A project manager must analyze the changes thoroughly before taking decisions related to changes to the project's plans are taken. Having a change control board helps in analyzing the impact on the project baselines. Based on the changes to the project*

> scope, we should change resource assignments, or maybe change the team structure and project organization. This all helps to keep the project on track with the desired project outcome'. Ponder and deliberate before you make a move.'

→ Disciplined and calm, to await the appearance of disorder and hubbub amongst the enemy; this is the art of retaining self-possession.

→ To refrain from intercepting an enemy whose banners are in perfect order, to refrain from attacking an army drawn up in calm and confident array—this is the art of studying circumstances.

→ Do not pursue an enemy who simulates flight; do not attack soldiers whose temper is keen.

→ Do not swallow bait offered by the enemy. Do not interfere with an army that is returning home.

> For a project manager, these statements highlight the importance of following defined change management process. *'Do not make changes to the plan baseline unless the changes are reviewed based on a defined change management process.'*

Sun Tzu, in the chapter, **VARIATION IN TACTICS**, reiterates and says that;

→ The general who thoroughly understands the advantages that accompany variation of tactics knows how to handle his troops.

The Comparison

- → The general who does not understand these may be well acquainted with the configuration of the country, yet he will not be able to turn his knowledge to practical account.

- → So, the student of war who is unversed in The Art of War of varying his plans, even though he be acquainted with the Five Advantages, will fail to make the best use of his men.

- → Hence in the wise leader's plans, considerations of advantage and of disadvantage will be blended together.

- → If our expectation of advantage be tempered in this way, we may succeed in accomplishing the essential part of our schemes.

- → If, on the other hand, in the midst of difficulties we are always ready to seize an advantage, we may extricate ourselves from misfortune.

> *'In a project management world, all these statements simply mean that, 'a project manager must keep the plans flexible, must devise a mechanism to manage changes, must have the ability to understand the importance of changing the plans and for the project's benefits.'*

Let's now examine similarities between *The Art of War* and the time management knowledge area in PMBOK®.

Reader's Notes

CHAPTER 6

Project Time Management

When we undertake a project, the plan should be the starting point. A plan is like a map that shows how we reach the destination—a completed project—as each individual task is completed. The basic essential data to have for the plan is the task duration, how long it will take to complete. That is directly related to the resources used, of course. In the larger picture, we also need to know how they relate to other tasks required in the project. It is important to know whether a task follows, precedes, or is accomplished in conjunction with other tasks.

One would need to know whether there are dependencies or if another project task cannot start until one finishes or if there are tasks that must start together or end together and so on. Start time, end time, duration, dependencies, and the owner or the responsible person(s) are the data that are also relevant. This is also one of the reasons why we need to define the scope of a project very clearly. This helps us to be able to communicate to our customer that we did understand their needs. Therefore, it should be communicated to the customer in terms as unambiguous as possible. It has a direct impact on the project planning and scheduling activities. The ability to understand the customers and their needs are thus of vital importance in drawing the project schedule.

On this time schedule, what is most crucial is the time estimate for each task and how that is affected by resource applications (increase/decrease). Like any structured activity, you start with a first cut estimates and then try refining the plan. It is vital to remember that the time schedule is not written in stone. Besides these initial iterations for refining the plan, the schedule can change as the project progresses and corrections are called for, depending on the actual progress of the tasks. An additional activity that relates to making the plans is communicating with all stakeholders in the plan. It is essential that you get buy-in from the project resources. Many times, particularly for new projects, time estimates depend largely on the experience of the people who estimate the tasks. So a process of review is essential. Besides, any organization will require multiple levels of approvals, starting with the project manager to several higher levels. Budgetary needs also dictate these levels of approval.

The managers want things to be done on time and budget. In their turn, their responsibility to investors is to get company projects done on time and within estimated costs. Missed deadlines are an embarrassment on agendas when communicating with investors, media, or customers and may not be acceptable at all. If project completion on time is important for the bosses, it is going to be very seriously important for your professional growth too. Managing the time schedule is the single most important activity toward achieving the on-time delivery of your projects. During the annual performance appraisal ritual, you can be sure time schedule management issues are going to top the agenda for discussion between you and the appraiser.

> *Similar to PMBOK®,* The Art of War *emphasizes defining activities, sequencing the activities, estimating the resources needed to perform the activities, developing a schedule, and, finally, controlling the schedule from the perspective of going to war. There is a lot of emphasis on sequencing of activities and the development of the schedule.*

The Comparison

Let us examine *The Art of War*, as against the processes in project Time Management.

6.1 Define Activities

Activity definition means to define the specific actions to perform to complete project deliverables. These are called activities and are the level beneath work packages. Scope baseline is an important piece of information that is needed to execute this process.

In *The Art of War* chapter, **TACTICAL DISPOSITIONS**, has following reference;

→ In respect of military method, we have, firstly, Measurement; secondly, Estimation of quantity; thirdly, Calculation; fourthly, Balancing of chances; fifthly, Victory

> These are examples of activities that are needed in the war. *'To plan for project success, it is important to define the activities to a more granular level. This involves the measurements, estimations, and calculations.'*

6.2 Sequence Activities

The purpose of sequencing activities is to identify and document the relationships between activities. This process can be performed with a PM tool, manually, or with a combination of both methods. Essentially, this process is about sequencing the tasks and activities in such a way that all internal and external dependencies are organized together in one work breakdown structure. Sun Tzu's views on sequencing the activities can be found in *The Art of War*.

Chapter **TACTICAL DISPOSITIONS**, has following;

→ Measurement owes its existence to Earth; Estimation of quantity to Measurement; Calculation to Estimation of quantity; Balancing of chances to Calculation; and Victory to Balancing of chances.

In chapter **WEAK POINTS AND STRONG POINTS**, Sun Tzu says that;

→ But if neither time nor place be known, then the left wing will be impotent to succor the right, the right equally impotent to succor the left, the van unable to relieve the rear, or the rear to support the van. How much more so if the furthest portions of the army are anything under a hundred Li apart, and even the nearest are separated by several Li.

> To a project manager, it serves as an example of *'importance of understanding the main activities and milestones that can have an impact on the project and carefully evaluating internal and external dependencies.'* This also means that, *'Without a proper determination of interdependence of activities, the project will be sure to face difficulties as it progresses.'*

→ How victory may be produced for them out of the enemy's own tactics—that is what the multitude cannot comprehend.

> Here, Sun Tzu, means that, *'a project can be successfully completed only when the intricate details are understood and related difficulties turn in project's favour. Therefore, it is must that the dependencies identified, sequenced and planned in the WBS.'*

The chapter, **THE ATTACK BY FIRE**, following statement appears that reads;

→ There is a proper season for making attacks with fire, and special days for starting a conflagration.

→ The proper season is when the weather is very dry; the special days are those when the moon is in the constellations of the Sieve, the Wall, the Wing, or the Cross-bar; for these four are all days of rising wind.

> Sun Tzu, again, is insisting on, *'Identifying the sequence and dependencies of the various activities. Additionally, Sun Tzu, also highlights the decision making ability of a project manager..*

6.3 Estimate Activity Resources

The purpose of this process is to estimate the type and quantities of resources required to perform each activity. This process must be performed in close coordination with the estimate cost process.

Chapter **MANEUVERING**, has a statement;

→ We may take it then that an army without its baggage-train is lost; without provisions it is lost; without bases of supply it is lost.

> It is an example of, *'Estimating the type and quantity of resources needed for performing activities'* and is obviously needed to ensure project success.

6.4 Estimate Activity Durations

In this process, a PM estimates the number of work periods required to complete individual activities. Information about the activity scope, required resource types, estimated resource quantities, and resource calendars are needed. This process is progressively elaborated on based on the available data.

In **MANEUVERING**, Sun Tzu observes that;

→ Thus, if you order your men to roll up their buff-coats and make forced marches without halting day or night, covering double the usual distance at a stretch, doing a hundred Li in order to wrest an advantage, the leaders of all your three divisions will fall into the hands of the enemy.

Chapter **WEAK POINTS AND STRONG POINTS** states;

→ If neither time nor place be known, then the left wing will be impotent to succor the right, the right equally impotent to succor the left, the van unable to relieve the rear, or the rear to support the van. How much more so if the furthest portions of the army are anything under a hundred Li apart, and even the nearest are separated by several Li!

> This means that, *'While planning a project and developing a schedule that the estimations are developed, activities are sequenced for the plan to work. This estimation helps not only in planning the project, but also in analyzing any impacts on the project schedule.'*

6.5 Develop Schedule

A project schedule is created based on activity sequences, durations, resource requirements, and schedule constraints. Essentially an iterative process, it determines the start and finish dates for project activities and milestones. Revise and maintain a schedule throughout the project as it progresses and as risk events unfold. In *The Art of War*, Sun Tzu states the following that relates to project schedule development.

Following are the quotes in chapter WEAK POINTS AND STRONG POINTS;

→ Knowing the place and the time of the coming battle, we may concentrate from the greatest distances in order to fight.

> Meaning, *'Insights into the project tasks, timelines, and dependencies enables appropriate planning and sequencing in the best possible manner so as to ensure project success.*

→ But if neither time nor place be known, then the left wing will be impotent to succour the right, the right equally impotent to succour the left, the van unable to relieve the rear, or the rear to support the van. How much more so if the furthest portions of the army are anything under a hundred Li apart, and even the nearest are separated by several Li!

> Though this statement appears in the process about estimation, with reference to schedule development, it means that, *'Determining and evaluating activities, milestones and dependencies are as important as estimating for them for the project's success'*

→ Military tactics are like unto water; for water in its natural course runs away from high places and hastens downwards.

→ So in war, the way is to avoid what is strong and to strike at what is weak.

> *'Sequence the project tasks on the path of least delay (the critical path) to create the project schedule e.g. Focussing on the tasks that have most dependencies downstream and completing the activities that take lesser time or have least dependencies on other tasks.'*

The chapter, **MANEUVERING**, quotes Sun Tzu that;

→ If you set a fully equipped army in march in order to snatch an advantage, the chances are that you will be too late. On the other hand, to detach a flying column for the purpose involves the sacrifice of its baggage and stores.

> Simple advice to the project manager that, *'Emphasizes the importance of resource estimation and task durations in development of project schedules.*

→ Thus, if you order your men to roll up their buff-coats, and make forced marches without halting day or night, covering double the usual distance at a stretch, doing a hundred Li in order to wrest an advantage, the leaders of all your three divisions will fall into the hands of the enemy.

→ The stronger men will be in front; the jaded ones will fall behind, and on this plan only one-tenth of your army will reach its destination.

- → If you march fifty Li in order to outmaneuver the enemy, you will lose the leader of your first division, and only half your force will reach the goal.
- → If you march thirty Li with the same object, two-thirds of your army will arrive.

> Sun Tzu in *The Art of War* goes further about scheduling and discusses scenarios that are best suitable as examples of schedule crashing and fast-tracking. *'Crashing and fast-tracking methods can be used to attain schedule compression and the relative tradeoffs and risks associated with it. Nonetheless, they remain powerful tools to compress the project schedule.'*

6.6 Control Schedule

The control schedule determines the status of the project schedule, identifies the schedule changes if changes have occurred, and influences and manages scheduling changes. In *The Art of War*, we come across the following few statements about control schedule process.

In chapter **WAGING WAR**, Sun Tzu says that;

- → Thus, though we have heard of stupid haste in war, cleverness has never been seen associated with long delays.
- → There is no instance of a country having benefited from prolonged warfare.

> Sun Tzu's advice is, *'To ensure, the success of the project, the schedule must be monitored and controlled to foresee*

and avoid delays. Long delays or longer projects cost more money and are more likely to be termed as failures.'

In **WEAK POINTS AND STRONG POINTS** chapter, we come across;

→ Water shapes its course according to the nature of the ground over which it flows; the soldier works out his victory in relation to the foe he is facing.

> *'Changes happen during the course of the project. A project manager should monitor the status of the project and must be flexible to change plans as needed to ensure the project's success. This culture should be imbibed in the team and team members must be a skilled resource to identify if changes to the existing plans are needed.'*

→ He who can modify his tactics in relation to his opponent, and thereby succeed in winning, may be called a heaven-born captain.

> Sun Tzu, in this statement, emphasizes on, *'The need to manage change as per a defined change management process. Existing baselines need to be changed based on dynamic conditions during the course of the project.'*

In the next chapter, we will see how *The Art of War*, is similar to the processes in the 'project cost management' knowledge area.

Reader's Notes

CHAPTER 7

Project Cost Management

Cost management consists of estimating, budgeting, and controlling costs. While skilled experts contribute a lot in cost estimations, a well-defined scope helps a lot in determining the project cost budgets.

The first major activity of cost management is to estimate the cost, clearly. Once the cost is determined, the efforts of management must be directed toward determining a budget, and an effort must be directed at maintaining the cost within that budget. Estimating is the sum of the cost approximations of various activities. The success of creating the budget depends on how accurately one is able to determine the exact activities. One of the standard problems is that any project activity is never a replica of what you might have done earlier. Only when the activities are similar can cost estimates are anywhere near actual costs. The budget estimates are an aggregation of cost estimates of various project activities and work packages and that help to arrive at a monetary ceiling. As definition these are by definition estimates, variances are always possible. The project manager has to keep an eagle eye on any significant variation from the cost baseline established by the budget. If variances happen, your plan must include ways to correct and prevent that.

The scope definition is critical here. To make a project outcome as deterministic as possible, we have to know exactly what needs to be done to achieve each outcome defined in the project scope. Project scope efforts are modified by the quality achievement targets set for the project by the organization and the project team.

Project scope defines what might be involved and the probable costs of material, activities, or the resources employed. It is at this initial stage that one could make decisions that influence costs. For smaller projects, the estimating and budgeting processes may be combined into one and handled by a single person.

A cost management plan establishes the formats to be used and the criteria for planning, structuring, estimating, budgeting, and controlling costs. Estimation of the cost is an approximation, and accuracy and confidence levels depend on how well we understand the process that accomplishes the activity.

> *Similar to PMBOK®,* The Art of War *discusses the need to estimate costs, determine and plan the budget, and take measures to control costs to ensure that a campaign does not strain the state. It discusses how wise generals control the costs to ensure success in battle, without putting the state exchequer at risk.*

We will now see the similarities between *The Art of War* and the 'project cost management' knowledge area.

7.1 Estimate Costs

The activity cost estimates in quantitative amounts are created and are usually stated in monetary units that reflect the cost of the resources needed to complete the project activities. These estimates are predictions based on information known at any given point in time. While estimating cost trade-offs between risks, make/buy, buy/lease play a major part. Though done during planning, cost estimation is an iterative process that gets refined from one phase to the next phase. Let's see what Sun Tzu said about cost estimation.

Chapter **WAGING WAR**, contains following few statements;

→ In the operations of war, where there are in the field a thousand swift chariots, as many heavy chariots, and a hundred thousand mail-clad soldiers, with provisions enough to carry them a thousand Li, the expenditure at home and at the front, including entertainment of guests, small items such as glue and paint, and sums spent on chariots and armor, will reach a total of a thousand ounces of silver per day. Such is the cost of raising an army of 100,000 men.

> This is inferred as *'Costs should be estimated for all resources that will be required to complete the project. This should cover all direct and indirect costs.'*

→ Bring war material with you from home, but forage on the enemy. Thus, the army will have food enough for its needs.

> Here, Sun Tzu has advised on optimization of the project cost. *'Develop an approximation of the monetary resources needed to complete the project activities. While estimating resources, analyze trade-offs and alternatives; use appropriate make versus buy, buy versus lease, or sharing of resources to achieve optimal costs for the project.'*

→ Hence a wise general makes a point of foraging on the enemy. One cartload of the enemy's provisions is equivalent to twenty of one's own, and likewise a single PICUL of his provender is equivalent to twenty from one's own store.

> *'A project manager must analyze trade-offs and alternatives while estimating resources and make appropriate plans; use appropriate make versus buy, buy versus lease, or sharing of resources to achieve optimal costs for the project.'*

7.2 Determine Budget

The process outcome is to develop a cost performance baseline based on aggregated estimated costs of individual activities in the work packages. This baseline is used while executing monitor and control processes to measure performance.

In the chapter, **WAGING WAR**, Sun Tzu says that;

→ On the other hand, the proximity of an army causes prices to go up; and high prices cause the people's substance to be drained away.

→ When their substance is drained away, the peasantry will be afflicted by heavy exactions.

→ With this loss of substance and exhaustion of strength, the homes of the people will be stripped bare, and three-tenths of their income will be dissipated; while government expenses for broken chariots, worn-out horses, breastplates and helmets, bows and arrows, spears and shields, protective mantles, draught-oxen, and heavy wagons will amount to four-tenths of its total revenue.

> *For a project manager, it means that, 'While cost estimation is available by now, the project manager must take into the environmental factors, the inherent assumptions, reserves*

Project Cost Management

and contingencies while determining the budget and finalizing a cost baseline.'

7.3 Control Costs

The purpose of controlling costs is monitoring project costs to prevent unauthorized or incorrect costs from being included in the cost baseline. This process is also used to make certain the budget isn't exceeded. The project status updates are monitored to manage any changes to the cost baselines by influencing the factors that create changes to the authorized cost baseline.

About cost control, in chapter **WAGING WAR**, Sun Tzu says that;

→ Again, if the campaign is protracted, the resources of the state will not be equal to the strain.

> A project manager must remember that, *'Delays in the schedule will have a bearing on resources. Earned Value Management (EVM) is an important tool to monitor and control project progress in terms of schedule and costs. EVM helps to monitor both work performance and cost performance.'*

→ The skillful soldier does not raise a second levy; neither are his supply-wagons loaded more than twice.

> Sun Tzu, in this statement, has commented on the importance of a project manager's skill level. *'It is only through the right level of knowledge and skills, a project manager can ensure that estimations are reasonably*

> *accurate. Through monitoring and controlling, a good project manager controls the project costs and readjusts the budget, whenever needed'.*

The intent of processes in quality management knowledge area, I found had some resemblance with some statements in *The Art of War*, in the next chapter.

Reader's Notes

CHAPTER 8

Project Quality Management

Quality is a fundamental requirement in any project. Quality indicates how the project is delivered. An incomplete scope definition or poorly articulated requirements lead to an unacceptable project/product. Consequently this situation results in a quality deficient project outcome. One of the first things one needs to remember about the quality of a project or product is that it can be obtained only by conscious design. Thus, like any other feature or deliverable, quality needs to be carefully managed so that the outcome is as designed. A complementary part of that statement is that quality is designed-in, and it cannot be inspected-in. Unless the quality is designed-in, the quality levels will be impossible to achieve irrespective of the rigor and method of the inspections.

The project quality management is three pronged. Firstly, quality must be planned. Quality assurance is the second prong of quality management, and the third prong of project quality management is quality control. At the quality planning stage, you look at the scope baseline and the stakeholder register. Cost performance and schedule baselines, risks, environmental factors, and organizational process assets are referred to create the quality management plan, metrics and checklists, quality improvement plan, and project document updates. Use the tools as necessary from the arsenal available, specific benchmarks, design of experiments, control charts, statistical sampling techniques, and anything unique to your organization and tools that apply in your context.

Though, the scope baseline, is one of the single most important factors in the quality planning, for an efficient and effective, quality management plan, stakeholder-related information such as needs and expectations, baselines for cost and schedule, as well as, the risks, threats, and possible mitigation and contingencies play a very important role.

There are several well-known experts who contributed to the development of quality management principles. Joseph M. Juran contributed to the quality discipline through his focus on cross-functional management processes. W. Edwards Deming contributed in the areas of statistical control and sampling. He popularized the plan-do-check-act cycle of Shewhart as a basic philosophy of quality management. His main argument was that as quality improves, costs reduce through less rework and waste. As a result of these principles, customer satisfaction rises and market share improves. Phillip B. Crosby was the proponent of the "doing it right the first time" or "zero defects" principle. Crosby was the proponent of the philosophies that the definition of quality is "conformance to requirements," "the system of quality is prevention," "the performance standard is zero defects," and "the measurement of quality is the price of non conformance."

Juran was successful in creating the awareness that organizational leadership has a role to play on quality of a team's product and services. He was of the opinion that unless these stakeholders drove the processes, quality management will not be effective and efficient. Deming and Crosby, too, subscribed to the theory that management has to be educated in quality principles and drive quality management. There are numerous tools, theories, and processes that are proposed and invented by many quality management gurus that will help a project manager in delivering the projects.

The Comparison

> *The Art of War tries to bring out the necessity of performing steps that bear similarities with quality management as defined in PMBOK®, to understand where the deficiencies are. The need for quality control and strict adherence to quality is emphasized to ensure the positions are made unassailable during war.*

War is mission critical, therefore; it is obvious we can find a few statements in *The Art of War* that relate to Quality Management.

8.1 Plan Quality

The activities in this process help a project manager identify quality requirements and standards needed in the project. An approved scope statement, details of major project deliverables, and acceptance criteria form the basis of the quality plan of a project. Information about stakeholders, project deliveries, risks, project baselines, and government regulations must be available prior to the approval of any quality plan. A Quality Plan is essentially a part of the project management plan.

Chapter **TACTICAL DISPOSITIONS**, of *The Art of War*, quote Sun Tzu;

→ He wins his battles by making no mistakes. Making no mistakes is what establishes the certainty of victory, for it means conquering an enemy that is already defeated.

> This relates directly to the Quality Management. *The outcome of a project has a direct impact on organizational strategic objectives. A project failure can lead stakeholders*

to question the strategic direction of the organization. The concepts of quality management help a project manager to assess the acceptance requirements of the project and prepare a quality plan for the project's success.

Chapter **VARIATION IN TACTICS**, contains one more quote;

→ The Art of War teaches us to rely not on the likelihood of the enemy's not coming, but on our own readiness to receive him; not on the chance of his not attacking, but rather on the fact that we have made our position unassailable.

For a project manager, it means that, *'The principles of quality management planning ensure that the project is planned in such a way that it is set up to meet success as a team is always ready and prepared.'*

8.2 Perform Quality Assurance

During the process of quality assurance, a PM makes certain that the project satisfies the quality standards laid out in the project management plan. The activities in this process provide a foundation for continuous process improvements, reducing waste and eliminating activities that do not add value.

In the chapter, **WEAK POINTS AND STRONG POINTS**, Sun Tzu observes;

→ Carefully compare the opposing army with your own, so that you may know where strength is superabundant and where it is deficient.

> *A project manager must use quality tools, perform quality audits to understand the team's strengths and weaknesses and use benchmarking to compare against industry standards for identifying areas for improvement.*

8.3 Perform Quality Control

The end product should conform to the requirements and product description defined during the planning processes. The activities in this process help in achieving these objectives. Results of executing the quality activities are checked, monitored, and recorded to evaluate performance and recommend necessary changes. This process was a bit tough to find similarities with the text in *The Art of War*.

In chapter, **TACTICAL DISPOSITIONS**, Sun Tzu stated;

→ He wins his battles by making no mistakes.

> This contains a very important message for the project manager. '*A project manager must monitor and record results of the project and utilize the processes, tools and techniques of quality control, to assess project performance as against project baselines. A project manager who with a keen eye of measurements will have higher chances project success.*'

→ The consummate leader cultivates the moral law and strictly adheres to method and discipline; thus it is in his power to control success.

In this quote, Sun Tzu says that, *'A project manager must strictly adhere to the project's defined processes. This not only results in transparency at the appropriate levels of the project organization, it brings predictability in the project results.'*

Projects and victories are fought by people and soldiers. Therefore, it was no surprise that there were similarities between both the texts as we will see in the next chapter, project human resources management.

Reader's Notes

CHAPTER 9

Project Human Resource Management

Human resources are a crucial part of the resources deployed in a project. The processes in this knowledge area help in assembling, building and managing a team on an ongoing basis. Identifying and locating resources, coupled with a recruitment plan are constituents of the team acquisition process. The assembled team goes through the process of forming, storming, and norming before it starts to perform as a team. That process takes time and careful nurturing. With not-so-perfect people availability, there may be training and development needs to be fulfilled.

Building a team and managing it should be part of the human resources plan of the project. Typical stages of such a plan would be to develop a human resources plan, acquire, develop and manage the team. The human resources plan would include identifying roles and responsibilities for the required positions. The necessary skills that go with that job description, structure of the team, and reporting relationships need to be defined unambiguously. A staffing management plan or mobilization plan of these resources, armed with descriptions and the team structure together helps create a human resources plan.

Several influencing factors need to be taken into consideration while preparing to build a team: organizational environment, structure, culture, marketplace conditions, skill requirements, politics of the organization and the region, location, existing human resources processes, and roles definition. The Human resource management plan must be clear about authority and responsibility. The team members should also be clear about what is not part of their responsibilities.

During the project execution, the project manager needs to monitor the performance of team members, provide feedback, resolve conflicts, resolve issues, and manage changes to optimize performance. These management processes are essential to ensure optimum team performance and to achieve project delivery. An integrated team is an imperative for the desired project outcome. During the project execution, as communication increases, there also exist countless opportunities for misunderstandings, conflicts, and ego clashes that can potentially lead to situations not desirable for the outcome of the project.

To keep a tab on motivation levels in the team and to ensure that every member of the team continues to operate at his or her best, the project manager can deploy a multitude of measures and employ some of the industry's most effective tools and best practices. While a disciplined and communicative team that works in a collaborative manner is a real asset to the organization, an undisciplined team hinders the project's progress. Building a high performing team is as critical as the expectations management, to ensure a successful project closure.

> *The Art of War* *places emphasis on teams rather than on individuals. The emphasis is on developing teams, keeping spirits up and keeping soldiers motivated. The role of the general in the creation of a strong, united army is stressed.* The Art of War *discusses rewards and recognition, and other incentives to motivate the army. Building the army into a single fighting unit and emphasizing teamwork rather than the individual is stressed many times.*

There are obvious similarities as we will see below, between both the texts, with regards to human resource management knowledge area.

9.1 Develop Human Resource Plan

This process helps a project manager identify project roles and responsibilities in order to create project organizational charts and the staff management plan. There are several influencing factors like organizational policies, technical needs, location, logistics, and regional politics that need to be considered while preparing a human resource management plan. There are two references in *The Art of War*, to human resource plan development process.

Sun Tzu, in chapter **ENERGY** states that;

→ The control of a large force is the same principle as the control of a few men: it is merely a question of dividing up their numbers.

> Meaning, *'Human resource planning is a key factor in project success. Determine and identify human resources with the necessary skills, and place them in smaller teams. In a larger project, make smaller teams and assign ownership and roles clearly in the project organization chart.'*

→ Fighting with a large army under your command is nowise different from fighting with a small one: it is merely a question of instituting signs and signals.

> A project manager must ensure that, *'A human resource plan provides guidance on how project human resources*

should be managed and controlled. The project organization chart, roles and responsibilities matrix make managing and controlling teams of any size relatively easier. The project structure and reporting relationships must be clear.'

9.2 Acquire Project Team

A project manager needs the resources to complete a project, and activities in this process help him to do so. Any failure to acquire necessary human resources affects project baselines, adds to the project risks, can potentially decrease the probability of success and may result in project cancellation. The project management team may have to negotiate with and influence the resource providers (individuals or groups). A PM may or may not have control over the number of team members or skills of those selected in the project.

The chapter **MANEUVERING**, in *The Art of War*, Sun Tzu makes a very powerful observation;

→ We are not fit to lead an army on the march unless we are familiar with the face of the country—its mountains and forests, its pitfalls and precipices, its marshes and swamps.

As we know that building a skilful team is necessary for the project's success, *'It is also necessary that the project manager himself has needed skills to steer the project successfully.'*

Sun Tzu, in **ATTACK BY STRATAGEM**, observes;

- → But when the army is restless and distrustful, trouble is sure to come from the other feudal princes. This is simply bringing anarchy into the army, and flinging victory away.

> *High team performance can be achieved by using open and effective communication to avoid conflicts, developing trust among team members, and managing conflicts in a constructive manner. Team conflicts, if not managed well, will lead to distrust and low morale. Such teams would be low performing and could potentially lead to project failure.*

- → Thus, we may know that there are five essentials for victory:
  - → (1) He will win who knows when to fight and when not to fight.
  - → (2) He will win who knows how to handle both superior and inferior forces.
  - → (3) He will win whose army is animated by the same spirit throughout all its ranks.

> *A good project manager will also have to be a good leader. He or she should be able to manage all stakeholders and have the ability to create high-performance teams. He or she has the ability to communicate the vision and inspires the team toward the common goal.*

In the chapter, **ENERGY**, he says,

- → The clever combatant looks to the effect of combined energy, and does not require too much from individuals, hence his ability to pick out the right men and utilize combined energy.

The Comparison

> *Teamwork is a critical factor for project success, and developing effective project teams is one of the primary responsibilities of the project manager. A project manager should create an environment that facilitates teamwork and should not rely too much on individual contributions.*

In the chapter, **MANEUVERING**, he says that;

→ When you plunder a countryside, let the spoil be divided amongst your men; when you capture new territory, cut it up into allotments for the benefit of the soldiery.

> *Engage in team-building activities. Celebrate project success with the team.*

→ Now a soldier's spirit is keenest in the morning; by noonday it has begun to flag; and in the evening, his mind is bent only on returning to camp.

> *Project team members are most enthusiastic during the execution stages of the project, when the team is going through it's norming and performing phase. When the project is nearing the end, team members are more worried about their future, and this worry can have an impact on the project. It is important that the project manager understands this, addresses concerns of the team and keeps them motivated.*

Project Human Resource Management

9.3 Manage Project Team

A project manager must track and review a team's performance, provide feedback, resolve conflicts, and issue and coordinate changes to enhance project performance. There may be complexities in doing this in a matrix organization when the team member is accountable to both the PM and the functional manager. This process helps a project manager carry out such tasks and not let's examine *The Art of War* and see what message it has to a project manager

In **WAGING WAR**, Sun Tzu comments on some more aspects of team acquisition;

→ When you engage in actual fighting, if victory is long in coming, then men's weapons will grow dull, and their ardor will be damped. If you lay siege to a town, you will exhaust your strength.

> Sun Tzu wanted a leader to ensure that, *'During the course of a project, especially in projects of long duration, it is important to keep the morale of the team high. Unusual delays and other issues can lead to lowered motivation. A motivated team in a two year long project is more important than in a project that is just three to six months long. Therefore, the project manager must accommodate team building and team effectiveness activities in the project plan.'*

→ Now, when your weapons are dulled, your ardor damped, your strength exhausted, and your treasure spent, other chieftains will spring up to take advantage of your extremity. Then no man, however wise, will be able to avert the consequences that must ensue.

> This statement, to a project manager, means, 'A project is in trouble when the team loses the motivation and focus. Developing effective project teams and keeping them focused and inspired is the duty of the project manager. The project managers must continually motivate their teams by providing challenges and opportunities.'

→ Now in order to kill the enemy, our men must be roused to anger; that there may be advantage from defeating the enemy, they must have their rewards.

> A project manager must motivate and inspire the team to work toward project success. Institute rewards and reward desirable behavior of the team members.

→ Therefore in chariot fighting, when ten or more chariots have been taken, those should be rewarded who took the first.

> 'Only desirable behavior should be rewarded. The team cannot be motivated to strive harder at work, if rewards are put for easily achievable deliverables, actions, and personal behaviour.'

In **ATTACK BY STRATAGEM**, Sun Tzu comments;

→ There are three ways in which a ruler can bring misfortune upon his army:

Project Human Resource Management

→ (1) By commanding the army to advance or to retreat, being ignorant of the fact that it cannot obey. This is called hobbling the army.

→ (2) By attempting to govern an army in the same way as he administers a kingdom, being ignorant of the conditions which obtain in an army. This causes restlessness in the soldiers' minds.

→ (3) By employing the officers of his army without discrimination, through ignorance of the military principle of adaptation to circumstances. This shakes the confidence of the soldiers.

Just like in a war, the results depend on the skillful army general, *'Successful projects require strong leadership skills. A project manager needs to possess strong management and leadership skills for creating high-performance teams. It is important to communicate the vision and inspire the team toward the common goal. The project manager should take into consideration the organizational structure, team dynamics, and other environmental factors while building and managing the team. Project managers must clearly articulate points and positions. Lack of these skills could lead to decreased team morale, low performing teams, and potential failure of the project.'*

Chapter **THE ARMY ON THE MARCH**, has following quotes;

→ If soldiers are punished before they have grown attached to you, they will not prove submissive; and, unless submissive, then will be practically useless. If, when the soldiers have become attached to you, punishments are not enforced, they will still be useless.

The Comparison

→ Therefore, soldiers must be treated in the first instance with humanity, but kept under control by means of iron discipline. This is a certain road to victory.

> Meaning that, *'During project team development, establish project performance evaluation criteria, rewards and recognition, and organizational policies with the team. The team should be aware of how they will be evaluated and what is expected. Managing a project team involves tracking its performance, providing feedback, and taking necessary actions as needed.'*

As we know communication plays an important part in the projects as you will see in the next chapter, Sun Tzu had some opinions that will help the project managers in managing teams.

Reader's Notes

CHAPTER 10

Project Communications Management

A communication management plan is a "never-to-forget" part of the project management. Depending on the stakeholders involved, need to communicate the essential information to the stakeholders can make project communications very complex. Therefore, meticulous planning in this area is absolutely vital. Unplanned and ad-hoc exercises in communicating can be disastrous.

Your communication plan needs to specify certain essential items. Some of these are about the information to be communicated; to whom, by whom, how often, what format, etc. These requirements include stakeholder communications requirements, language, format, content, and level of detail to be released. Reason for distribution should also be described in order to get the desired effect out of the distributed information. The person authorized to release and distribute information and the names of the person(s) authorized to receive the information need to be put down on the plan, along with frequency of information distribution.

A project is always a niche activity. Thus, a specific project may not affect all of the visible and well-known stakeholders. It needs careful analysis to arrive at a list of stakeholders affected by a particular project. This analysis for identifying those affected by a process or an event is known as the stakeholder analysis. While it is essential that the specific stakeholders be identified, it is also essential to note their interests, their involvement, and their impact on the success of the project. That would ensure that the stakeholders get communications that are tailored to their needs. Nobody wants to or has the time to wade through a mass of information that has something for everyone.

When you have a large number of stakeholders with varied needs for information, managing the communication process can get very complicated indeed. What you need is a clear management strategy to ensure every information need of these stakeholders is met. Any non trivial project will have enough combinatorial variations that it would be easy to miss the communication process required to meet the information need of someone. Unless there is a formal management strategy to meet this need, there will be communication gaps. The only way to avoid gaps is to set up processes that ensure nothing is missed.

When you distribute information, it has to be properly organized rather than distributing raw data. Thus, while there may be lots of discrete inputs related to the performance of the project, the information you distribute should make the project progress transparent and must clearly indicate if the project is on track.

There are several other dimensions of the communication process. These are formal or informal, vertical or horizontal. Communication can happen in any or in a combination of more than one form of these. Formal communication is usually through regularly issued written or printed reports and newsletters. Oral communication can be verbal or nonverbal, quite often the two together convey the real meaning of the information.

As the project manager, you will need to exercise a host of communication skills that are important for not only project communications, but also, in general, in most other corporate roles. Being able to listen is probably the top-of-the-chart skill, you are going to need. Fact-finding skills that allow you to identify and confirm the information is important. The ability to exercise logic, to probe, question, and establish the facts is needed.

> *In wars, as in projects, poor communication can result in disaster.* The Art of War *emphasizes the need for communications, for planning information needs and methods of information distribution, and for making these available to all generals, and soldiers. There are references to how information distribution happens and the various ways of reporting performance. These are similar to PMBOK® steps in communications management, though given mainly in the context of the battle and battlefield situations.*

10.1 Identify Stakeholders

Stakeholders are customers, sponsors, performing organization, public, and anyone who is impacted positively or negatively by the project щгесщьу. The stakeholder identification process assists the project manager in identifying and documenting stakeholders' interests. A project manager should also devise a plan to deal with potential negative impacts of the project outcome. Organizational structure, culture, industry standards, and government policies are some of the influencing factors that should be taken into consideration. We have some insights from *The Art of War*, about this process, as well.

Sun Tzu, in chapter **ATTACK BY STRATAGEM**, says that;

→ In the practical art of war, the best thing of all is to take the enemy's country whole and intact; to shatter and destroy it is not so good. So, too, it is better to recapture an army entire than to destroy it, to capture a regiment, a detachment, or a company entire than to destroy them.

→ Hence to fight and conquer in all your battles is not supreme excellence; supreme excellence consists in breaking the enemy's resistance without fighting.

→ Thus, the highest form of generalship is to thwart the enemy's plans.

→ The rule is not to besiege walled cities if it can possibly be avoided.

→ Therefore, the skillful leader subdues the enemy's troops without any fighting; he captures their cities without laying siege to them; he overthrows their kingdom without lengthy operations in the field.

> The victory without battle is the least expensive for the state, and it also demands a thorough understanding of the enemy's design. *'This strategy implies that to deliver an acceptable project outcome, the project manager must understand the stakeholders' needs and interests. A cost-efficient outcome needs understanding of several possible solution and execution approaches.'*

The chapter, **TERRAIN**, has quote;

→ We may distinguish six kinds of terrain, to wit:

(1) accessible ground, (2) entangling ground, (3) temporizing ground, (4) narrow passes, (5) precipitous heights, and (6) positions at a great distance from the enemy.

> *In a similar vein, PMBOK implies that good understanding of the project environment assists a project manager in strategizing and applying suitable execution approaches to any project.*

10.2 Plan Communications

The activities necessary for this process help a project manager in ensuring timely and appropriate Generation, Collection, Distribution, Storage, Retrieval, and Disposition of project information. It is imperative to take into consideration the stakeholders' needs and interests and to develop communication strategies to ensure information requirements are met.

In **MANEUVERING**, Sun Tzu says the following about communication planning;

→ On the field of battle, the spoken word does not carry far enough: hence the institution of gongs and drums. Nor can ordinary objects be seen clearly enough: hence the institution of banners and flags.

→ Gongs and drums, banners and flags are means whereby the ears and eyes of the host may be focused on one particular point.

> By this, Sun Tzu means that, *'Information needs and methods of information distribution should be carefully considered. Use appropriate communication technology and communication models for effective information distribution. Communication methods should be clearly outlined in the Communications Management Plan and made available to all stakeholders.'*

10.3 Distribute Information

It is a process of making relevant information available to the relevant project stakeholders. This process involves implementing the communications management plan and responding to ad-hoc requests for information. Building consensus and overcoming disagreements and resistance are critical factors to be considered.

In the chapter about **MANEUVERING**, Sun Tzu discussed the importance of sending the right information to the soldiers and said that;

→ In night-fighting, then, make much use of signal-fires and drums, and in fighting by day, of flags and banners, as a means of influencing the ears and eyes of your army.

> In a project, it can be applied as, *'Distribute information as defined in the communications management plan. This will help the stakeholders to understand the information better, which in turn will help them to formulate their own plans.'*

10.4 Manage Stakeholder Expectations

This is a process of communicating and working with stakeholders, to meet their needs, address and resolve issues as they occur, and influence their expectations. It involves actively managing expectations to identify risks and to increase the probability of project acceptance. The project manager is responsible for stakeholder expectations management to build trust and decrease the risk that the project will fail to meet the project's goals and objectives. About expectations management, Sun Tzu has some brief and profound insights,

In the chapter about **MANEUVERING**, he says that;

→ In war, the general receives his commands from the sovereign.

And chapter **VARIATION IN TACTICS**, contains following quotes;

→ There are roads which must not be followed, armies which must be not attacked, towns which must be besieged, positions which must not be contested, and commands of the sovereign which must not be obeyed.

> This, to a project manager carries a meaning that, 'A *project manager is expected to receive work and orders from his senior executives and stakeholders. However, the project manager's primary responsibility is to understand their expectations from the project's outcome. Sometimes it may also mean not to obey the orders from the senior executives and stakeholders. The project manager must be careful in discussing and communicating with the stakeholders.'*

10.5 Report Performance

This process helps the project manager in collecting and distributing performance information, including status reports, progress measurements, and forecasts. It involves the periodic collection and analysis of baseline versus actual data to understand and communicate progress, performance, and forecasted results. A report is never complete without stating the risks and issues, the analysis of variances to the project baselines, the progress made so far, and the next actions planned. I found that reporting the progress and communication in *The Art of War*, is given an important place. Consider the following quotes of Sun Tzu.

In the chapter, **THE ARMY ON THE MARCH**, Sun Tzu has said;

→ Movement among the trees of a forest shows that the enemy is advancing. The appearance of a number of screens in the midst of thick grass means that the enemy wants to make us suspicious.

→ The rising of birds in their flight is the sign of an ambuscade. Startled beasts indicate that a sudden attack is coming.

→ When there is dust rising in a high column, it is the sign of chariots advancing; when the dust is low, but spread over a wide area, it betokens the approach of infantry. When it branches out in different directions, it shows that parties have been sent to collect firewood. A few clouds of dust moving to and fro signify that the army is encamping.

→ Humble words and increased preparations are signs that the enemy is about to advance. Violent language and driving forward as if to attack are signs that he will retreat.

→ When the light chariots come out first and take up a position on the wings, it is a sign that the enemy is forming for battle.

→ Peace proposals unaccompanied by a sworn covenant indicate a plot.

~~~~~~~~~~~~~~~~~~~~~~~~~~~~~~~~

The various statements above show that, through proper reporting, risks and issues can be identified earlier. *'Project reporting is not only a project manager's job, but also that of the team members, provided the team feels empowered to report problems and challenges. It is important to conduct a periodic collection and analysis of project progress, as well as the current status of risks and issues. Information about project performance and the current status of risks and issues should be communicated as defined in the Communications Management Plan. Information should be collected and transmitted in such a way that the receiver of the information can decipher*

> *the information correctly. Using reporting formats like dashboards or traffic light reporting can sometimes clearly communicate status and alert stakeholders to risks and issues.'*

The next chapter, project risk management, is about the similarities between the risk management knowledge area and *The Art of War*.

Reader's Notes

CHAPTER 11

Project Risk Management

In an entirely predictable system, there are no risks involved because the "unknowns" do not exist. The response to these unknowns can result in either negative or positive outcome. Therefore, some of the risks can actually turn out to be positive risks that open up further opportunities.

Theoretically at least, if the project-planning process can enumerate and take care of all the potential threats, there are no risks. The only problem that can happen is if you have overlooked something and planned actions are not known. However, any real-life project is a far more complex system in which it is not possible to know everything with certainty. Whenever there is an element of uncertainty, there is a risk involved that the event may affect your project adversely. In any real-life project, there are many factors that can produce an event with a negative impact on your project—from the unpredictable behavior of a team member, to delayed supplies from a vendor, or even the vendor going bankrupt.

One needs to be able to identify all such risks. What needs to be done is to have a contingency plan for every one of these identified risks. At least, then, you are sure that if the event does strike, at least cost alternatives are available. The biggest problem is identifying all possible risks in a project. You'll need to start by identifying all the areas where things can go wrong. This would be a tool in focusing your thoughts on the risk areas and making sure you are able to think up most of the risks. Typically internal or external events, organizational issues, or even project management plan can give rise to risks. A project manager cannot think of all the potential problems; hence, it is necessary to involve all the team members. In a multidisciplinary project, the project teams' expertise and experience would help to enhance risk identification and mitigation process.

The risk-management plan identifies the initial set of risks, a management plan for the risks, and a process by which project progress will be monitored. It also reflects an awareness that the risk scenario can change as the project progresses. The manager must watch out for new threats, and planning should include processes for analyzing new threats and for carrying out mitigation. The analysis of risk in both qualitative and quantitative terms helps to develop practical mitigation processes.

Risk planning is a process through which one enumerates risk management activities related to the project. Defining and documenting the activities ensures that they are followed consistently throughout the duration of the project. Risk identification begins by identifying risks as foreseen at the start. You could start by setting up a risk breakdown structure that is like a mind map. It will help to focus on areas that are likely to give rise to risks.

The outcome of a qualitative risk analysis is to make a qualitative assessment of the impact of the identified risks. That helps the project management team to assign a relative priority easily. As with any other resource constrained situation, this prioritization is essential and helps deploy resources optimally. Risk probability analysis and the impact assessment, in terms of impact on the project outcome such as schedule, cost, quality, and performance, need to be determined. Any positive aspect arising out of risks can be looked at as opportunities. The risk response needs to specify applying resources and initiating activities according to budget, schedule, and project management perspectives and the relative priorities of the risk. The qualitative and quantitative assessment helps in prioritizing risk responses, in the risk response plan.

Risk monitoring and control are ongoing tasks, where a project manager is always on the lookout for threats and problems. The proactive process of watching for risks quite often helps in taking preventive measures ahead of problems coming up. One way of doing this is to conduct trend and variance analzes on the project performance on an ongoing basis. A continuous reality check to verify that project assumptions remain valid, to assess whether risks have changed, to see that risk management policies are being followed, or if cost reserves need to be modified, also helps.

> *Similar to PMBOK®,* The Art of War *puts great emphasis on the need to identify risks. Identifying risks and determining the risks that can affect the outcome of the battle is the major responsibility of the general (much as in PMBOK®). There are some discussions around risk analysis, and there is great emphasis on planning risk responses.* The Art of War *lays great emphasis on various risk mitigation strategies and planning appropriate risk responses to deal with all the identified risks. There is also emphasis on monitoring and controlling risks throughout the course of the battle, very similar to how risk is addressed in PMBOK®.*

Stakes are high in battles and wars. Therefore, in the following discussions you will find that much of the book, *The Art of War,* is dedicated to managing risks during the war.

11.1 Plan Risk Management

This process guides a project manager in defining the mechanisms and means to conduct risk management activities for a project. The Risk Management Plan determines how to plan for risks, and this plan becomes an agreed-upon baseline for evaluating project risks. Project scope, cost, schedule, stakeholders' powers, needs, their interests, organizational cultures, organizational structures has the most influence on project risks. Sun Tzu, in his book, has given indications about how a general should carefully study the environment, army's march and the enemy movements to perceive the risks.

11.2 Identify Risks

This process is meant to determine the risks and to document their characteristics. The risks are ranked for further analysis and response. While identifying the risks, one must take into account the stakeholders, scope, project baselines, and organizational policies and culture.

In chapter **ENERGY**, Sun Tzu says that;

→ Simulated disorder postulates perfect discipline, simulated fear postulates courage; simulated weakness postulates strength.

→ Hiding order beneath the cloak of disorder is simply a question of subdivision; concealing courage under a show of timidity presupposes a fund of latent energy; masking strength with weakness is to be effected by tactical dispositions.

> Which implies, *'Identify risks and determine which risks may affect the project. Risk identification involves using the entire project team and drawing from its experience*

> *(expert judgment) as well as several tools and techniques. If risks are not properly identified and recorded, the chances of risks becoming issues during the course of the project will be higher.'*

In the chapter, **THE ARMY ON THE MARCH**, Sun Tzu says;

→ These are the four useful branches of military knowledge which enabled the Yellow Emperor to vanquish several sovereigns.

→ All armies prefer high ground to low and sunny places to dark.

→ If you are careful of your men and camp on hard ground, the army will be free from disease of every kind, and this will spell victory.

→ When you come to a hill or a bank, occupy the sunny side, with the slope on your right rear. Thus, you will at once act for the benefit of your soldiers and utilize the natural advantages of the ground.

→ When, in consequence of heavy rains up-country, a river which you wish to ford is swollen and flecked with foam, you must wait until it subsides.

→ If in the neighborhood of your camp there should be any hilly country, ponds surrounded by aquatic grass, hollow basins filled with reeds, or woods with thick undergrowth, they must be carefully routed out and searched; for these are places where men in ambush or insidious spies are likely to be lurking.

Project Risk Management

> *These statements imply that, 'Identify risks and determine which risks may affect the project and document their characteristics. Proper risk identification, and analysis of their characteristics are needed to plan appropriate risk responses. Use a variety of methods and tools like SWOT, expert judgment in identifying risks.'*

Lastly, in the chapter, **THE USE OF SPIES**, Sun Tzu says;

→ Thus, what enables the wise sovereign and the good general to strike and conquer, and achieve things beyond the reach of ordinary men, is foreknowledge.

> This is about communication, and to a project manager, it means that, *'It is important to have information about all types of potential risks in a project. It is only possible to manage risks if we have appropriate details of information and knowledge about all possible risks to the project delivery. Such an approach will enhance the chances of project success..'*

11.3 Perform Qualitative Risk Analysis

Qualitative Risk Analysis is the process of prioritizing risks for analysis or action by assessing and combining their probability and impact. This is a rapid, cost-effective means of establishing priorities for Plan Risk Responses. It lays the foundation for further actions and processes in risk management of the project.

About qualitative risks analysis, in chapter **WEAK POINTS AND STRONG POINTS**, Sun Tzu has said that,

→ Though the enemy is stronger in numbers, we may prevent him from fighting. Scheme so as to discover his plans and the likelihood of their success.

> This statement implies that, *'Once risks are identified, perform a qualitative risk analysis. Assess the relative probability or likelihood of occurrence of the identified risks along with the chance of their success, and the corresponding impact on project objectives if they occur. This qualitative analysis can help the project team be better prepared and plan appropriate risk responses.'*

11.4 Perform Quantitative Risk Analysis

The activities in this process help in the evaluation of the impacts of the prioritized risk and quantify the risk exposure by assigning numeric probabilities to each risk and its impact on project objectives. They help in quantitatively determining the probability of achieving the project outcomes and objectives. The activities help identify realistic and achievable schedules, cost, or scope targets. They determine the best project management decisions possible when outcomes are uncertain. The modern management science thrives on numbers and we can find tons of meaningful tools and some jargon as well, on this topic. What surprised me that *The Art of War*, had also a statement that resembled with quantitative analysis.

In chapter, **WEAK POINTS AND STRONG POINTS**, Sun Tzu says;

→ But if neither time nor place be known, then the left wing will be impotent to succor the right, the right equally impotent to succor the left, the van unable to relieve the rear, or the rear to support the van. How much more so if the furthest portions of the army are anything under a hundred Li apart, and even the nearest are separated by several Li.

> This advice implies that *'Any impact of the potential threat to the project outcome, cannot be analzed in its entirety unless, the potential threat is analzed quantitatively. It is difficult to predict the project outcome without the basic data about the threats, and hence the project success is likely to be unpredictable.*

11.5 Plan Risk Responses

This process helps a project manager to describe the suitable response to identified risks, such as avoid, transfer, mitigate, accept, exploit, share, enhance, create contingent strategies, and apply expert judgment in developing options and actions to enhance opportunities and to reduce threats to project objectives. Let's now see the similarities between *The Art of War* and this process.

In **ATTACK BY STRATAGEM**, *The Art of War*, has following quotes;

→ Thus, the highest form of generalship is to thwart the enemy's plans; the next best is to prevent the junction of the enemy's forces; the next in order is to attack the enemy's army in the field, and the worst policy of all is to besiege walled cities.

> Implying that, *'Develop options and actions to reduce threats to the project objectives and enhance opportuni-*

> ties. As part of planning risk responses, a project manager should identify strategies for positive risks or opportunities as well as strategies for negative risks or threats.'

→ The rule is not to besiege walled cities if it can be avoided. The preparation of mantles, movable shelters, and various implements of war will take up three whole months; and the piling up of mounds over against the walls will take three months more.

> This admonition can be interpreted as avoiding certain risks to eliminate the threat entirely. Avoiding the risk can help prevent costly escalations of schedule delays and isolate the project objectives from the risk's impact.

Chapter **TACTICAL DISPOSITIONS**, contains this statement;

→ Hence the skillful fighter puts himself into a position which makes defeat impossible.

> This sentence implies that, 'A good project manager reduces threats to project objectives by planning risk responses.'

Chapter **ENERGY**, quotes;

→ To ensure that your whole host may withstand the brunt of the enemy's attack and remain unshaken—this is effected by maneuvers direct and indirect.

> This statement indicates that, *'Right mitigation strategies can void risk of any magnitude. Use risk analysis tools to choose the most appropriate responses. A strategy or mix of strategies most likely to be effective should be selected for each risk.'*

Sun Tzu, in the chapter, **WEAK POINTS AND STRONG POINTS**, states that;

→ You may advance and be absolutely irresistible, if you make for the enemy's weak points; you may retire and be safe from pursuit if your movements are more rapid than those of the enemy.

→ If we wish to fight, the enemy can be forced to an engagement even though he be sheltered behind a high rampart and a deep ditch. All we need to do is attack some other place that he will be obliged to relieve.

→ If we do not wish to fight, we can prevent the enemy from engaging us even though the lines of our encampment be merely traced out on the ground. All we need to do is to throw something odd and unaccountable in his way.

> *'The risks may have an impact on the outcome of the project, but the project's success is influenced by the responses to the risks, therefore, a PM should develop options and actions to reduce threats and enhance opportunities for the project's success objectives.'*

The Comparison

Chapter **VARIATION IN TACTICS**, contains some more statements about risk response planning;

→ The Art of War teaches us to rely, not on the likelihood of the enemy's not coming, but on our own readiness to receive him; not on the chance of his not attacking, but rather on the fact that we have made our position unassailable.

> This has a direct implication for a project manager. *'Only a proactive approach in risk management can lead you to the project's success. A risk with higher impact and lower probability, if occurs can lead you to massive failure, without any response planning in place. A project manager must be prepared to deal with all potential obstacles.'*

→ When in difficult country, do not encamp. In country where high roads intersect, join hands with your allies. Do not linger in dangerously isolated positions. In hemmed-in situations, you must resort to stratagem. In desperate positions, you must fight.

→ There are roads which must not be followed, armies which must be not attacked, towns which must not be besieged, positions which must not be contested, and commands of the sovereign which must not be obeyed.

→ Reduce the hostile chiefs by inflicting damage on them; and make trouble for them, and keep them constantly engaged; hold out specious allurements, and make them rush to any given point.

> Some examples of risk response planning. *'While a risk can be transferred by allying with a partner, it can totally*

be avoided by abandoning the activity that results in risk to occur. The third statement above, is an example of using mitigation as a response to the risk.'

In **THE ARMY ON THE MARCH**, more about risk responses is found;

- → Camp in high places, facing the sun. Do not climb heights in order to fight. So much for mountain warfare.

- → After crossing a river, you should get far away from it.

- → When an invading force crosses a river in its onward march, do not advance to meet it in midstream. It will be best to let half the army get across, and then deliver your attack.

- → If you are anxious to fight, you should not go to meet the invader near a river which he has to cross.

- → Moor your craft higher up than the enemy and facing the sun. Do not move upstream to meet the enemy. So much for river warfare.

- → In crossing salt-marshes, your sole concern should be to get over them quickly, without any delay.

- → If forced to fight in a salt-marsh, you should have water and grass near you, and get your back to a clump of trees. So much for operations in salt-marshes.

- → In dry, level country, take up an easily accessible position with rising ground to your right and on your rear, so that the danger may be in front, and safety lie behind. So much for campaigning in flat country.

- → A country in which there are precipitous cliffs with torrents running between, deep natural hollows, confined places,

The Comparison

> tangled thickets, quagmires and crevasses should be left with all possible speed and not approached.

→ While we keep away from such places, we should get the enemy to approach them; while we face them, we should let the enemy have them on his rear.

Chapter **TERRAIN**, also has Sun Tzu's quotes on responses to threats;

→ In a position of this sort, even though the enemy should offer us attractive bait, it will be advisable not to stir forth, but rather to retreat, thus enticing the enemy in his turn; then, when part of his army has come out, we may deliver our attack with advantage.

→ With regard to narrow passes, if you can occupy them first, let them be strongly garrisoned and await the advent of the enemy.

→ Should the army forestall you in occupying a pass, do not go after him if the pass is fully garrisoned, but only if it is weakly garrisoned.

→ With regard to precipitous heights, if you are beforehand with your adversary, you should occupy the raised and sunny spots, and there wait for him to come up.

→ If the enemy has occupied them before you, do not follow him, but retreat and try to entice him away.

These statements are indications that, 'The project manager must adopt a proactive approach. They also serve as examples of responses to different types of challenges and obstacles. Once the risks are identified, plan an appropriate risk response to deal with the identified risks. A PM should adopt a strategy that reduces the threat and enhances op-

portunities to deliver projects successfully. All such details must be documented in the risk register.'

11.6 Monitor and Control Risks

The monitoring and controlling risks, is a process of implementing risk response plans, tracking risks, monitoring residual risks, identifying new risks, and evaluating risk process effectiveness throughout the project. Project variance and trend analysis are used extensively during this process. Additionally it also involves evaluating fallback plans, validity of assumptions, risk closure, and re-estimation of contingency reserves. *The Art of War* teaches a lot about risk management and this process about risk monitoring is no different.

Sun Tzu, in **ATTACK BY STRATAGEM**, says that;

→ The general, unable to control his irritation, will launch his men to the assault like swarming ants, with the result that one-third of his men are slain, while the town still remains untaken. Such are the disastrous effects of a siege.

> *'Monitor and control risks by tracking identified risks and evaluating risk process effectiveness throughout the project. Always stay on top of the risks, and duly follow planned risk responses to avoid costly mishaps during the project. Rushed responses are a No-Go.'*

In the chapter, **WEAK POINTS AND STRONG POINTS**, quotes Sun Tzu;

→ An army may march great distances without distress if it marches through country where the enemy is not.

> This quote from *The Art of War* contains a significant message for the project manager, 'Highlighting the significance of risk responses. When the risk is managed appropriately and proactively, the project team makes significant progress during the course of the project. Project risk assessments should be done regularly to avoid risks from occurring.'

The chapter, **THE ARMY ON THE MARCH**, quotes;

→ When the enemy is close at hand and remains quiet, he is relying on the natural strength of his position.

→ If his place of encampment is easy of access, he is tendering a bait.

→ Movement among the trees of a forest shows that the enemy is advancing. The appearance of a number of screens in the midst of thick grass means that the enemy wants to make us suspicious.

→ The rising of birds in their flight is the sign of an ambuscade. Startled beasts indicate that a sudden attack is coming.

→ When there is dust rising in a high column, it is the sign of chariots advancing; when the dust is low, but spread over a wide area, it betokens the approach of infantry. When it branches out in different directions, it shows that parties have been sent to collect firewood. A few clouds of dust moving to and fro signify that the army is encamping.

→ Humble words and increased preparations are signs that the enemy is about to advance. Violent language and driving forward as if to the attack are signs that he will retreat.

- When the light chariots come out first and take up a position on the wings, it is a sign that the enemy is forming for battle.
- Peace proposals unaccompanied by a sworn covenant indicate a plot.
- When there is much running about and the soldiers fall into rank, it means that the critical moment has come.
- When some are seen advancing and some retreating, it is a lure.
- When the soldiers stand leaning on their spears, they are faint from want of food.
- If those who are sent to draw water begin by drinking themselves, the army is suffering from thirst.
- If the enemy sees an advantage to be gained and makes no effort to secure it, the soldiers are exhausted.
- If birds gather on any spot, it is unoccupied. Clamor by night betokens nervousness.
- If there is disturbance in the camp, the general's authority is weak. If the banners and flags are shifted about, sedition is afoot. If the officers are angry, it means that the men are weary.
- When an army feeds its horses with grain and kills its cattle for food, and when the men do not hang their cooking-pots over the campfire, showing that they will not return to their tents, you may know that they are determined to fight to the death.
- The sight of men whispering together in small knots or speaking in subdued tones points to disaffection among the rank and file.

→ Too frequent rewards signify that the enemy is at the end of its resources; too many punishments betray a condition of dire distress.

→ To begin by bluster but afterwards to take fright at the enemy's numbers shows a supreme lack of intelligence.

→ When envoys are sent with compliments in their mouths, it is a sign that the enemy wishes for a truce.

→ If the enemy's troops march up angrily and remain facing ours for a long time without either joining battle or taking themselves off again, the situation is one that demands great vigilance and circumspection.

→ If our troops are no more in number than the enemy, that is amply sufficient; it only means that no direct attack can be made. What we can do is simply to concentrate all our available strength, keep a close watch on the enemy, and obtain reinforcements.

> It is a long list of examples and says that, *'Monitor and control risks by tracking identified risks, implementing risk response plans, monitoring residual risks, identifying new risks, and evaluating risk process effectiveness through the project. Track identified risks to see if they occur, and monitor the risk responses to evaluate their effectiveness. Project work should be continuously monitored for new, changing, and outdated risks.'*

The last knowledge area, project procurement management, is not addressed in *The Art of War*. Nevertheless, there are few similarities in both the texts as we will see in the next chapter

Reader's Notes

CHAPTER 12

Project Procurement Management

The project related procurement process is quite an involved one and has four distinct stages. The project managers must be familiar with the procurement processes and must be able to deal with complexities that can arise due to project related procurements. The procurement processes are about both sides of the deal. The related processes must manage the buying of items, components, and possibly services from others. Similar processes must exist in an organization that will manage the related aspects of supplying a product or services to a buyer organization. The ongoing project may be the outcome of the efforts to provide these to the buyer. Plan procurements, conduct procurements, administer procurements and close the procurements are the four different and distinct processes on which the complete procurement process rests.

A plan for procurement needs to document the purchase needs, all the requirements in terms of specifications of the items, and approach, for procuring and identifying, the sellers. When conducting the procurements, the stages one has to go through are 1) obtaining responses from potential sellers, 2) selecting one out of the responding vendors, and 3) maybe awarding a contract to the selected supplier. The contracted supplies are not delivered instantly, therefore, planning and control activities are involved. These activities form part of administering the procurement process: managing the relationship set up through the contract, checking whether the contract is performing the right way and implementing changes and corrections as necessary. Getting a closure on the procurement activities forms the fourth and the last step of the full procurement management process. Though these processes are separate, you will find a lot of interactions and overlap between them.

The procurement planning process needs a range of inputs that must be considered to create a concrete plan. These include the project scope baseline, requirements documents, teaming agreements, the risk register, risk-related contract decisions, activity resource requirements, the schedule, cost estimates, and the cost performance baseline to name a few. Organizational environmental factors and an organization's process assets bring the specific context of the organization and the collective learning of the organization into the plans/decisions made in the process. The scope and the requirements documents help decide what products or services will need to be obtained from external sources.

Expertise that can help you make such "make or buy" decisions—including knowledge about the different types of contracts—should be used as appropriate. The procurement-management plan is produced as part of this exercise along with a specific statement of work (SOW) for each item to be procured. Make or buy decisions are documented, as are procurement documents and source-selection criteria. Change requests, if any, complete the documents created in this process.

Conducting procurements is the process of actually distributing the request for proposal (RFP), soliciting responses from potential suppliers, and then narrowing the choice and selecting one for the supply of the item. One may use a vendor conference to explain the needs and obtain responses. The RFP may be distributed to qualified vendors, and their responses obtained. In either process, an evaluation of vendor proposals is made to arrive at a "short list." Vendor conferences may even be conducted after responses to the request for quotation (RFQs) have been received. Vendors are then asked to quote their best possible terms.

The Comparison

Administering procurements is the process of nurturing the process, making sure contractual terms are observed, and making sure the supply happens in due course along with everything that needs to be done to ensure these goals.

Closing procurement ensures that the procurement is completed. This process also has to make sure that all deliverables by the supplying agency are acceptable.

> *There is very little discussion around the procurement management part in Sun Tzu's book, perhaps because of the nature of war compared to modern projects. Though suppliers might have existed even in the time of Sun Tzu, they are more likely to be under the control of kings and kingdoms; therefore no mention about them can be found in* The Art of War. *Given the fact that a supplier exists to complement some skills or products that our organization does not own, a supplier is necessarily an extension of the project team and, a supplier's activity could be planned and managed based on the project needs. The quotes of* The Art of War *that are applicable for planning, quality control, scope verification, and cost management can also be applied in procurement management.*

12.1 Plan Procurements

This process discusses the preparation of SOW and procurement documents and determining source selection criteria. It involves the activities needed for documenting project purchasing decisions, specifying the approach, and identifying potential sellers. Scope baselines, risks, cost estimates, marketplace conditions, organization policies, and guidelines are a few of the most common influencing factors in this process. This is the only process in procurement management, where we can find a similarity between both the texts.

Sun Tzu, in chapter, **MANEUVERING**, says that;

→ We cannot enter into alliances until we are acquainted with the designs of our neighbors.

> For a project manager, *'Planning procurements involve determining whether to acquire outside support, and if so, identifying potential vendors, and should also include due consideration of potential vendors to determine the degree of influence or control that can be exercised with the vendor.'*

12.2 Conduct Procurements

In this process, seller responses are obtained in the form of bids and proposals. Proposals are evaluated against the evaluation criteria, sellers or vendors are selected, and contracts are awarded. The team applies the agreed and defined selection criteria to select one or more sellers who are accepted as suppliers and are qualified to perform the work.

> In this process as well, no direct reference could be found in *The Art of War*. 'Nevertheless, the text from Chapter 11, *The Nine Situations*, discusses the internal and external environment situations that have influence on supplier selection decisions.'

12.3 Administer Procurements

This process deals with managing procurement relationships, monitoring the contract performance and making changes and corrections as needed. The process ensures that sellers performances meet procurement requirements and that the buyer performs according to the terms of the legal contract.

> Sun Tzu does not discuss the aspects of a partner's performance in his treatise. 'Nevertheless, when partners and vendors are considered to be part of the team, all the statements that deal with managing a project team, communication management, cost management, and alliances can be applied to this process.'

12.4 Close Procurements

The project manager completes each of the project procurements while performing the activities in this process. This process includes processes needed to close a project or phase and involves verification confirming that all work and deliverables were acceptable, completed accurately, and satisfactorily.

> No direct reference to contract closure is found in *The Art of War*, due to the reasons discussed above. 'However, the statements that are applicable to scope verification can also be applied to this process as the intent is similar.'

After having compared *The Art of War* with all the knowledge areas defined in the Project Management Body of Knowledge®, we will see, in the next chapter, how we can go beyond the PMBOK® and learn from *The Art of War*, what PMBOK® does not cover.

Reader's Notes

CHAPTER 13

Beyond PMBOK®

In this military classic that was written thousands of years ago and has been known to the locals ever since, I found that almost all of its ideas could be of great use to a project manager. The conflicting needs and interests of the stakeholders are the root of conflicts, and a project manager is expected to balance them. The skills, insight, and wisdom needed to contain the resulting organizational power games and politics, however, is not in the scope of PMBOK®. Often a project manager is faced with a situation in which a slight mistake may result in dire consequences for some of the stakeholders. The existence of sharks and wolves is also very well known in the corporate world. Sometimes, there are deliberate attempts to send ambiguous messages among employees to cause confusion and conflict. At times, a project manager finds himself in a position in which he has to handle a steering committee that acts like an assassination committee. PMBOK® does discuss the process and influence of the enterprise environment over project outcomes; *The Art of War* actually makes a very clear case for instilling a sense of discipline in the team. Sun Tzu clearly states the importance of secrecy and distributing based on the situation. Making such decisions requires wisdom and insight. Sun Tzu clearly advocates shorter campaigns that lead to quick wins in *The Art of War*.

PMBOK® discusses processes and lays out a framework and methodology that has proven to be successful in helping project managers and organizations alike. However, PMBOK® discusses the processes and offers advice on several tools and techniques to execute the processes. In a project, when the project manager faces issues, advice on handling such conflicts is out of the scope of PMBOK®. Sun Tzu discusses his ideas about focusing on shorter projects and quick wins, lays out advice about leadership, threat perceptions, strategies of defence, and eventually avoiding conflicts that will help a project manager to manage conflicts before they arise.

The corporate culture has encouraged competitiveness among its employees. A competitive culture helps an organization improve and can also lead to innovative ideas. On the flip side, it also results in a situation in which one has to deal with peer rivals. Some of the ideas in this book are very clear about how one can deal with these situations without creating any conflicts. Sun Tzu discusses at length the "grounds of the battle" on which the army has to meet the enemy's army. This discussion is one of the most powerful texts that anyone can ever read about analyzing the environment under which one has to operate.

Sun Tzu also discusses the assessment one should make when faced with a conflict between rivals. When in this situation, one must assess the strengths, the weaknesses, the support system within the organization, the rival's skills that can benefit the project, and, most importantly, whether a competitor or rival has some unique skills that can influence the project's outcome positively. If so, then one must work to use his skills to the project's maximum advantage. A good project manager does not let personal relationships influence the project's outcome.

Sun Tzu also emphasized the importance of a general adapting to work within constraints. The same applies to the project manager as he or she also has limited resources at his or her disposal and therefore, must use available resources creatively for optimum cost advantages.

The Comparison

Some of the ideas that go beyond PMBOK® are described in this chapter. The messages hidden in these statements are important to the project manager, some of them being *'survival-critical'* requirements to the project manager's job.

In the chapter, **LAYING PLANS**, following can be found;

→ Which of the two sovereigns is imbued with the Moral Law?

→ Which of the two generals has most ability?

→ With whom lie the advantages derived from Heaven and Earth?

→ On which side is discipline most rigorously enforced?

→ Which army is stronger?

→ On which side are officers and men more highly trained?

→ In which army is there the greater faithfulness both in reward and punishment?

→ By means of these seven considerations I can forecast victory or defeat.

> *'A project's positive outcome depends on many factors that can influence it deeply. Examples of these factors include the organization's culture for succeeding in projects; management's philosophy; the project manager's skill; the use of time and resources; the management structure created in the project; the performing organization's strengths and weaknesses; whether the managers and workers are trained; and suitable salaries.'*

- → All warfare is based on deception.

- → Hence, when able to attack, we must seem unable; when using our forces, we must seem inactive; when we are near, we must make the enemy believe we are far away; when far away, we must make him believe we are near.

- → Hold out baits to entice the enemy. Feign disorder, and crush him.

- → If he is secure at all points, be prepared for him. If he is in superior strength, evade him.

- → If your opponent is of choleric temper, seek to irritate him. Pretend to be weak, that he may grow arrogant.

- → If he is taking his ease, give him no rest. If his forces are united, separate them.

- → Attack him where he is unprepared; appear where you are not expected.

- → These military devices, if they lead to victory, must not be divulged beforehand.

> 'These lines suggest that, in competitive situations, one must find ways to control information to succeed. In addition to being familiar with project management principles and techniques, it is also necessary to be strategic to operate in the competitive business environments. It becomes imperative to control information and use information to your competitive advantage. Not acting decisively on a few occasions is as important as acting decisively when the time is right. You can succeed by focusing your limited resources on advancing along the path of least resistance.'

The Comparison

In the chapter, **WAGING WAR**, Sun Tzu says;

→ Our own flags should be substituted for those of the enemy and their chariots mingled and used in conjunction with ours. The captured soldiers should be kindly treated and kept.

→ This is called using the conquered foe to augment one's own strength.

> *'Learn to make success pay for itself. Use successes to augment the project execution capabilities. Do the same for lessons learned, knowledge bases, reusable components and materials, etc.'*

→ In war, then, let your great object be victory, not lengthy campaigns.

> *'Avoid long and expensive projects. Define smaller projects instead.'*

The chapter, **ENERGY**, quotes that;

→ There are no more than five musical notes, yet the combinations of these five give rise to more melodies than can ever be heard.

→ There are no more than five cardinal tastes (sour, acrid, salt, sweet, bitter), yet combinations of them yield more flavors than can ever be tasted.

> *'Any project has limited resources at its disposal. However, these limited resources can be mixed, combined and rearranged to come up with better ways to get the work done while using limited resources. There is no limit to the ways you can improve, therefore, It may never be possible to discover the possible ways project resources can be utilized. Similarly, there could be many ways to improve existing processes.'*

→ In battle, there are no more than two methods of attack—the direct and the indirect; yet these two in combination give rise to an endless series of maneuvers.

→ The direct and the indirect lead on to each other in turn. It is like moving in a circle—you never come to an end. Who can exhaust the possibilities of their combination?

> *'When dealing with projects, you rely on standard and innovative methods. You can use both and move from one to the other. The combination of these two gives you many options to choose from, and you never run out of options.'*

WEAK POINTS AND STRONG POINTS, mentions the following;

→ For should the enemy strengthen his van, he will weaken his rear; should he strengthen his rear, he will weaken his van; should he strengthen his left, he will weaken his right; should he strengthen his right, he will weaken his left. If he sends reinforcements everywhere, he will everywhere be weak.

> *'Every organization has an infinite number of needs but limited resources. It is important that you choose the needs that can best be addressed by the limited resources.'*

And the chapter, **TERRAIN**, quotes;

→ If you know the enemy and know yourself, your victory will not stand in doubt; if you know Heaven and know Earth, you may make your victory complete.

> *'Knowing your strengths and weaknesses will clearly improve your chances of project success. Knowledge of the business environment and the ground business realities further enhances your chances to attain project success.'*

Sun Tzu, in the chapter, **THE NINE SITUATIONS**, observes that;

→ The Art of War recognizes nine varieties of ground: (1) dispersive ground; (2) facile ground; (3) contentious ground; (4) open ground; (5) ground of intersecting highways; (6) serious ground; (7) difficult ground; (8) hemmed-in ground; and (9) desperate ground.

→ When a chieftain is fighting in his own territory, it is dispersive ground.

→ When he has penetrated into hostile territory but to no great distance, it is facile ground.

→ Ground which, if possessed, imports great advantage to either side is contentious ground.

- → Ground on which each side has liberty of movement is open ground.

- → Ground that forms the key to three contiguous states, so that he who occupies it first has most of the empire at his command, is a ground of intersecting highways.

- → When an army has penetrated into the heart of a hostile country, leaving a number of fortified cities in its rear, it is serious ground.

- → Mountain forests, rugged steeps, marshes and fens—all country that is hard to traverse: this is difficult ground.

- → Ground that is reached through narrow gorges and from which we can retire only by tortuous paths—so that a small number of the enemy would suffice to crush a large body of our men—this is hemmed-in ground.

- → Ground on which we can be saved from destruction only by fighting without delay is desperate ground.

- → On dispersive ground, therefore, fight not. On facile ground, halt not. On contentious ground, attack not.

- → On open ground, do not try to block the enemy's way. On the ground of intersecting highways, join hands with your allies.

- → On serious ground, gather in plunder. In difficult ground, keep steadily on the march.

- → On hemmed-in ground, resort to stratagem. On desperate ground, fight.

> To a project manager, it means, '*A project manager must be able to identify, know when the work environment is divisive, easy, competitive, open, shared, risky, bad,*

restricting, or desperate. Projects could be experiencing one or more of these work environments during the course of a project's Lifecycle. To find success in divisive environments, it is important to discourage opposition. In easy environments, encourage everyone to keep going. In competitive environments, discourage internal battles. In open environments, keep everybody working together. In shared environments, encourage partnerships. In risky environments, support the most productive people. In bad environments, consider changing the existing rules. In restricting environments, change the strategy and allow for innovation and creativity. In desperate environments, encourage your people to succeed.'

Section I of the book ends here.

Section II is the reader's free copy *The Art of War*.

Reader's Notes

SECTION II
Sun Tzu's *The Art of War*

Each and every concept in *The Art of War*, has, the capability to reduce conflicts and improve project outcomes.

CHAPTER 14

Laying Plans

1. *The Art of War* is of vital importance to the state.

2. It is a matter of life and death, a road either to safety or to ruin. Hence it is a subject of inquiry that can on no account be neglected.

3. *The Art of War*, then, is governed by five constant factors to be taken into account in one's deliberations when seeking to determine the conditions in the field.

4. These are: (1) The Moral Law; (2) Heaven; (3) Earth; (4) the commander; (5) method and discipline.

5. The MORAL LAW causes the people to be in complete accord with their ruler so that they will follow him regardless of their lives, undismayed by any danger.

6. HEAVEN signifies night and day, cold and heat, times and seasons.

7. EARTH comprises distances, great and small; danger and security; open ground and narrow passes; the chances of life and death.

8. The commander stands for the virtues of wisdom, sincerity, benevolence, courage, and strictness.

9. Method and discipline are to be understood as the marshaling of the army in its proper subdivisions, the graduations of rank among the officers, the maintenance of roads by which

supplies may reach the army, and the control of military expenditures.

10. These five heads should be familiar to every general: he who knows them will be victorious; he who knows them not will fail.

11. Therefore, in your deliberations, when seeking to determine the military conditions, let these be made the basis of a comparison.

   (1) Which of the two sovereigns is imbued with the Moral Law?

   (2) Which of the two generals has the most ability?

   (3) With whom lie the advantages derived from Heaven and Earth?

   (4) On which side is discipline most rigorously enforced?

   (5) Which army is stronger?

   (6) On which side are officers and men more highly trained?

   (7) In which army is there the greater faithfulness both in reward and punishment?

12. The general that hearkens to my counsel and acts upon it will conquer; let such a one be retained in command. The general that hearkens not to my counsel nor acts upon it will suffer defeat; let such a one be dismissed.

13. While heeding the profit of my counsel, avail yourself also of any helpful circumstances over and beyond the ordinary rules.

14. One should modify one's plans according to the favorability of circumstances.

15. All warfare is based on deception.

16. Hence, when able to attack, we must seem unable; when using our forces, we must seem inactive; when we are near, we must make the enemy believe we are far away; when far away, we must make him believe we are near.

17. Hold out baits to entice the enemy. Feign disorder, and crush him.

18. If he is secure at all points, be prepared for him. If he is in superior strength, evade him.

19. If your opponent is of choleric temper, seek to irritate him. Pretend to be weak, that he may grow arrogant.

20. If he is taking his ease, give him no rest.

21. Attack him where he is unprepared; appear where you are not expected.

22. These military devices, if they lead to victory, must not be divulged beforehand.

23. Now the general who wins a battle makes many calculations in his temple before the battle is fought.

CHAPTER 15

Waging War

1. In the operations of war, where there are in the field a thousand swift chariots, as many heavy chariots, and a hundred thousand mail-clad soldiers,

2. When you engage in actual fighting, if victory is long in coming, then men's weapons will grow dull and their ardor will be damped. If you lay siege to a town, you will exhaust your strength.

3. Again, if the campaign is protracted, the resources of the state will not be equal to the strain.

4. Now, when your weapons are dulled, your ardor damped, your strength exhausted and your treasure spent, other chieftains will spring up to take advantage of your extremity. Then no man, however wise, will be able to avert the consequences that must ensue.

5. Thus, though we have heard of stupid haste in war, cleverness has never been seen associated with long delays.

6. There is no instance of a country having benefited from prolonged warfare.

7. Only one who is thoroughly acquainted with the evils of war can thoroughly understand the profitable way of carrying it on.

8. The skillful soldier does not raise a second levy, neither are his supply wagons loaded more than twice.

9. Bring war material with you from home, but forage on the enemy. Thus, the army will have food enough for its needs.

10. The poverty of the state exchequer causes an army to be maintained by contributions from a distance.

11. On the other hand, the proximity of an army causes prices to go up; and high prices cause the people's substance to be drained away.

12. When their substance is drained away, the peasantry will be afflicted by heavy exactions.

13. With this loss of substance and exhaustion of strength, the homes of the people will be stripped bare, and three-tenths of their income will be dissipated.

14. Hence a wise general makes a point of foraging on the enemy. One cartload of the enemy's provisions is equivalent to twenty of one's own, and likewise a single PICUL of his provender is equivalent to twenty from one's own store.

15. Now in order to kill the enemy, our men must be roused to anger; that there may be advantage from defeating the enemy, they must have their rewards.

16. Therefore in chariot fighting, when ten or more chariots have been taken, those should be rewarded who took the first. Our own flags should be substituted for those of the enemy, and the chariots mingled and used in conjunction with ours. The captured soldiers should be kindly treated and kept.

17. This is called using the conquered foe to augment one's own strength.

18. In war, then, let your great object be victory, not lengthy campaigns.

19. Thus, it may be known that the leader of armies is the arbiter of the people's fate, the man on whom it depends whether the nation shall be in peace or in peril.

CHAPTER 16

Attack by Stratagem

1. In the practical art of war, the best thing of all is to take the enemy's country whole and intact; to shatter and destroy it is not so good. So, too, it is better to recapture an army entire than to destroy it, to capture a regiment, a detachment, or a company entire than to destroy them.

2. Hence, to fight and conquer in all your battles is not supreme excellence; supreme excellence consists in breaking the enemy's resistance without fighting.

3. Thus, the highest form of generalship is to thwart the enemy's plans.

4. The rule is not to besiege walled cities if it can possibly be avoided.

5. The general, unable to control his irritation, will launch his men to the assault like swarming ants.

6. Therefore, the skillful leader subdues the enemy's troops without any fighting; he captures their cities without laying siege to them; he overthrows their kingdom without lengthy operations in the field.

7. With his forces intact, he will dispute the mastery of the empire, and thus, without losing a man, his triumph will be complete.

8. It is the rule in war, if our forces are ten to the enemy's one, to surround him; if five to one, to attack him.

9. If equally matched, we can offer battle.

10. Hence, though an obstinate fight may be made by a small force, in the end it must be captured by the larger force.

11. Now the general is the bulwark of the state; if the bulwark is complete at all points, the state will be strong; if the bulwark is defective, the state will be weak.

12. There are three ways in which a ruler can bring misfortune upon his army:

    (1) By commanding the army to advance or to retreat, being ignorant of the fact that it cannot obey. This is called hobbling the army.

    (2) By attempting to govern an army in the same way as he administers a kingdom, being ignorant of the conditions which obtain in an army. This causes restlessness in the soldiers' minds.

    (3) By employing the officers of his army without discrimination, through ignorance of the military principle of adaptation to circumstances. This shakes the confidence of the soldiers.

13. But when the army is restless and distrustful, trouble is sure to come from the other feudal princes. This is simply bringing anarchy into the army and flinging victory away.

14. Thus we may know that there are five essentials for victory:

    (1) He will win who knows when to fight and when not to fight.

    (2) He will win who knows how to handle both superior and inferior forces.

(3) He will win whose army is animated by the same spirit throughout all its ranks.

(4) He will win who, prepared himself, waits to take the enemy unprepared.

(5) He will win who has military capacity and is not interfered with by the sovereign.

15. Hence the saying, If you know the enemy and know yourself, you need not fear the result of a hundred battles. If you know yourself but not the enemy, for every victory gained you will also suffer a defeat.

16. If you know neither the enemy nor yourself, you will succumb in every battle.

CHAPTER 17

Tactical Dispositions

1. The good fighters of old first put themselves beyond the possibility of defeat and then waited for an opportunity of defeating the enemy.

2. To secure ourselves against defeat lies in our own hands, but the opportunity of defeating the enemy is provided by the enemy himself.

3. Thus, the good fighter is able to secure himself against defeat but cannot make certain of defeating the enemy.

4. Hence the saying, One may know how to conquer without being able to do it.

5. Security against defeat implies defensive tactics; ability to defeat the enemy means taking the offensive.

6. Standing on the defensive indicates insufficient strength; attacking, a superabundance of strength.

7. The general who is skilled in defense hides in the most secret recesses of the earth; he who is skilled in attack flashes forth from the topmost heights of heaven. Thus, on the one hand, we have the ability to protect ourselves; on the other, a victory that is complete.

8. To see victory only when it is within the ken of the common herd is not the acme of excellence.

9. Neither is it the acme of excellence if you fight and conquer and the whole empire says, "Well done!"

10. To lift an autumn hair is no sign of great strength.

11. What the ancients called a clever fighter is one who not only wins, but excels in winning with ease.

12. Hence, his victories bring him neither reputation for wisdom nor credit for courage.

13. He wins his battles by making no mistakes.

14. Hence, the skillful fighter puts himself into a position which makes defeat impossible and does not miss the moment for defeating the enemy.

15. Thus it is that in war the victorious strategist seeks battle only after the victory has been won, whereas he who is destined to defeat first fights and afterwards looks for victory.

16. The consummate leader cultivates the moral law, and strictly adheres to method and discipline; thus, it is in his power to control success.

17. In respect of military method, we have, firstly, measurement; secondly, estimation of quantity; thirdly, calculation; fourthly, balancing of chances; fifthly, victory.

18. Measurement owes its existence to earth; Estimation of quantity to measurement; calculation to estimation of quantity; balancing of chances to calculation; and victory to balancing of chances.

19. A victorious army opposed to a routed one is as a pound's weight placed in the scale against a single grain.

20. The onrush of a conquering force is like the bursting of pent-up waters into a chasm a thousand fathoms deep.

CHAPTER 18

Energy

1. The control of a large force is the same principle as the control of a few men: it is merely a question of dividing up their numbers.

2. Fighting with a large army under your command is nowise different from fighting with a small one: it is merely a question of instituting signs and signals.

3. To ensure that your whole host may withstand the brunt of the enemy's attack and remain unshaken—this is effected by maneuvers direct and indirect.

4. That the impact of your army may be like a grindstone dashed against an egg—this is effected by the science of weak points and strong.

5. In all fighting, the direct method may be used for joining battle, but indirect methods will be needed in order to secure victory.

6. Indirect tactics, efficiently applied, are inexhaustible as heaven and earth, unending as the flow of rivers and streams; like the sun and moon, they end but to begin anew; like the four seasons, they pass away to return once more.

7. There are no more than five musical notes, yet the combinations of these five give rise to more melodies than can ever be heard.

8. There are no more than five primary colors (blue, yellow, red, white, and black), yet in combination they produce more hues than can ever been seen.

9. There are no more than five cardinal tastes (sour, acrid, salt, sweet, bitter), yet combinations of them yield more flavors than can ever be tasted.

10. In battle, there are no more than two methods of attack—the direct and the indirect; yet these two in combination give rise to an endless series of maneuvers.

11. The direct and the indirect lead on to each other in turn. It is like moving in a circle—you never come to an end. Who can exhaust the possibilities of their combination?

12. The onset of troops is like the rush of a torrent which will even roll stones along in its course.

13. The quality of decision is like the well-timed swoop of a falcon which enables it to strike and destroy its victim.

14. Therefore, the good fighter will be terrible in his onset and prompt in his decision.

15. Energy may be likened to the bending of a crossbow; decision, to the releasing of a trigger.

16. Amid the turmoil and tumult of battle, there may be seeming disorder and yet no real disorder at all; amid confusion and chaos, your array may be without head or tail, yet it will be proof against defeat.

17. Simulated disorder postulates perfect discipline; simulated fear postulates courage; simulated weakness postulates strength.

18. Hiding order beneath the cloak of disorder is simply a question of subdivision.

19. Thus, one who is skillful at keeping the enemy on the move maintains deceitful appearances, according to which the enemy will act.

20. By holding out baits, he keeps him on the march; then with a body of picked men, he lies in wait for him.

21. The clever combatant looks to the effect of combined energy and does not require too much from individuals.

22. When he utilizes combined energy, his fighting men become as it were like unto rolling logs or stones. For it is the nature of a log or stone to remain motionless on level ground and to move when on a slope; if four-cornered, to come to a standstill, but if round-shaped, to go rolling down.

23. Thus, the energy developed by good fighting men is as the momentum of a round stone rolled down a mountain thousands of feet in height. So much on the subject of energy.

CHAPTER 19

Weak Points and Strong Points

1. Whoever is first in the field and awaits the coming of the enemy will be fresh for the fight; whoever is second in the field and has to hasten to battle will arrive exhausted.

2. Therefore, the clever combatant imposes his will on the enemy but does not allow the enemy's will to be imposed on him.

3. By holding out advantages to him, he can cause the enemy to approach of his own accord, or by inflicting damage, he can make it impossible for the enemy to draw near.

4. If the enemy is taking his ease, he can harass him;

5. Appear at points which the enemy must hasten to defend; march swiftly to places where you are not expected.

6. An army may march great distances without distress, if it marches through country where the enemy is not.

7. You can be sure of succeeding in your attacks if you attack only places that are undefended.

8. Hence that general is skillful in attack whose opponent does not know what to defend; and he is skillful in defence whose opponent does not know what to attack.

9. O divine art of subtlety and secrecy! Through you we learn to be invisible, through you inaudible;

Weak Points and Strong Points

10. You may advance and be absolutely irresistible if you make for the enemy's weak points; you may retire and be safe from pursuit if your movements are more rapid than those of the enemy.

11. If we wish to fight, the enemy can be forced to an engagement though he be sheltered behind a high rampart and a deep ditch. All we need to do is attack some other place that he will be obliged to relieve.

12. If we do not wish to fight, we can prevent the enemy from engaging us even though the lines of our encampment be merely traced out on the ground. All we need to do is to throw something odd and unaccountable in his way.

13. By discovering the enemy's dispositions and remaining invisible ourselves, we can keep our forces concentrated, while the enemy's must be divided.

14. We can form a single united body, while the enemy must split up into fractions. Hence there will be a whole pitted against separate parts of a whole, which means that we shall be many to the enemy's few.

15. And if we are able thus to attack an inferior force with a superior one, our opponents will be in dire straits.

16. The spot where we intend to fight must not be made known; for then the enemy will have to prepare against a possible attack at several different points; and his forces being thus distributed in many directions, the numbers we shall have to face at any given point will be proportionately few.

17. For should the enemy strengthen his van, he will weaken his rear; should he strengthen his rear, he will weaken his van; should he strengthen his left, he will weaken his right; should he strengthen his right, he will weaken his left. If

he sends reinforcements everywhere, he will everywhere be weak.

18. The numerical weakness comes from having to prepare against possible attacks, numerical strength from compelling our adversary to make these preparations against us.

19. Knowing the place and the time of the coming battle, we may concentrate from the greatest distances in order to fight.

20. But if neither time nor place be known, then the left wing will be impotent to succor the right, the right equally impotent to succor the left, the van unable to relieve the rear, or the rear to support the van. How much more so if the furthest portions of the army are anything under a hundred Li apart, and even the nearest are separated by several Li!

21. Though according to my estimate the soldiers of Yueh exceed our own in number, that shall advantage them nothing in the matter of victory. I say then that victory can be achieved.

22. Though the enemy be stronger in numbers, we may prevent him from fighting. Scheme so as to discover his plans and the likelihood of their success.

23. Rouse him, and learn the principle of his activity or inactivity.

24. Carefully compare the opposing army with your own so that you may know where strength is superabundant and where it is deficient.

25. In making tactical dispositions, the highest pitch you can attain is to conceal them; conceal your dispositions, and you will be safe from the prying of the subtlest spies, from the machinations of the wisest brains.

26. How victory may be produced for them out of the enemy's own tactics—that is what the multitude cannot comprehend.

27. All men can see the tactics whereby I conquer, but what none can see is the strategy out of which victory is evolved.

28. Do not repeat the tactics which have gained you one victory, but let your methods be regulated by the infinite variety of circumstances.

29. Military tactics are like unto water; for water in its natural course runs away from high places and hastens downwards.

30. So in war, the way is to avoid what is strong and to strike at what is weak.

31. Water shapes its course according to the nature of the ground over which it flows; the soldier works out his victory in relation to the foe he is facing.

32. Therefore, just as water retains no constant shape, so in warfare there are no constant conditions.

33. He who can modify his tactics in relation to his opponent and thereby succeed in winning may be called a heaven-born captain.

34. The five elements (water, fire, wood, metal, earth) are not always equally predominant; the four seasons make way for each other in turn. There are short days and long; the moon has its periods of waning and waxing.

CHAPTER 20

Maneuvering

1. In war, the general receives his commands from the sovereign.

2. Having collected an army and concentrated his forces, he must blend and harmonize the different elements thereof before pitching his camp.

3. After that comes tactical maneuvering, than which there is nothing more difficult. The difficulty of tactical maneuvering consists in turning the devious into the direct and misfortune into gain.

4. Thus, to take a long and circuitous route, after enticing the enemy out of the way, and though starting after him, to contrive to reach the goal before him, shows knowledge of the artifice of deviation.

5. Maneuvering with an army is advantageous; with an undisciplined multitude, most dangerous.

6. If you set a fully equipped army in march in order to snatch an advantage, the chances are that you will be too late. On the other hand, to detach a flying column for the purpose involves the sacrifice of its baggage and stores.

7. Thus, if you order your men to roll up their buff-coats and make forced marches without halting day or night, covering double the usual distance at a stretch, doing a hundred Li in order to wrest an advantage, the leaders of all your three divisions will fall into the hands of the enemy.

8. The stronger men will be in front; the jaded ones will fall behind, and on this plan only one-tenth of your army will reach its destination.

9. If you march fifty Li in order to outmaneuver the enemy, you will lose the leader of your first division, and only half your force will reach the goal.

10. If you march thirty Li with the same object, two-thirds of your army will arrive.

11. We may take it then that an army without its baggage train is lost; without provisions it is lost; without bases of supply it is lost.

12. We cannot enter into alliances until we are acquainted with the designs of our neighbors.

13. We are not fit to lead an army on the march unless we are familiar with the face of the country—its mountains and forests, its pitfalls and precipices, its marshes and swamps.

14. We shall be unable to turn natural advantage to account unless we make use of local guides.

15. In war, practice dissimulation, and you will succeed.

16. Whether to concentrate or to divide your troops must be decided by circumstances.

17. Let your rapidity be that of the wind, your compactness that of the forest.

18. In raiding and plundering be like fire.

19. Let your plans be dark and impenetrable as night, and when you move, fall like a thunderbolt.

20. When you plunder a countryside, let the spoil be divided among your men; when you capture new territory, cut it up into allotments for the benefit of the soldiery.

21. Ponder and deliberate before you make a move.

22. He will conquer who has learned the artifice of deviation.

23. Such is the art of maneuvering.

24. On the field of battle, the spoken word does not carry far enough: hence the institution of gongs and drums. Nor can ordinary objects be seen clearly enough: hence the institution of banners and flags.

25. Gongs and drums, banners and flags, are means whereby the ears and eyes of the host may be focused on one particular point.

26. The host thus forming a single united body is it impossible either for the brave to advance alone, or for the cowardly to retreat alone. This is the art of handling large masses of men.

27. In night-fighting, then, make much use of signal-fires and drums, and in fighting by day, of flags and banners, as a means of influencing the ears and eyes of your army.

28. A whole army may be robbed of its spirit.

29. Now a soldier's spirit is keenest in the morning.

30. A clever general, therefore, avoids an army when its spirit is keen but attacks it when it is sluggish and inclined to return. This is the art of studying moods.

31. Disciplined and calm, to await the appearance of disorder and hubbub among the enemy—this is the art of retaining self-possession.

32. To be near the goal while the enemy is still far from it, to wait at ease while the enemy is toiling and struggling, to be well-fed while the enemy is famished—this is the art of husbanding one's strength.

33. To refrain from intercepting an enemy whose banners are in perfect order, to refrain from attacking an army drawn up in calm and confident array—this is the art of studying circumstances.

34. It is a military axiom not to advance uphill against the enemy, nor to oppose him when he comes downhill.

35. Do not pursue an enemy who simulates flight; do not attack soldiers whose temper is keen.

36. Do not swallow bait offered by the enemy.

37. Do not interfere with an army that is returning home.

38. When you surround an army, leave an outlet free. Do not press a desperate foe too hard.

39. Such is *The Art of Warfare*.

CHAPTER 21

Variation in Tactics

1. In war, the general receives his commands from the sovereign, collects his army, and concentrates his forces.

2. When in difficult country, do not encamp. In country where high roads intersect, join hands with your allies. Do not linger in dangerously isolated positions. In hemmed-in situations, you must resort to stratagem. In desperate positions, you must fight.

3. There are roads which must not be followed, armies which must be not attacked, towns which must not be besieged, positions which must not be contested, and commands of the sovereign which must not be obeyed.

4. The general who thoroughly understands the advantages that accompany variation of tactics knows how to handle his troops.

5. The general who does not understand these may be well acquainted with the configuration of the country, yet he will not be able to turn his knowledge to practical account.

6. So, the student of war who is unversed in *The Art of War* of varying his plans, even though he be acquainted with the Five Advantages, will fail to make the best use of his men.

7. Hence, in the wise leader's plans, considerations of advantage and of disadvantage will be blended together.

8. If our expectation of advantage be tempered in this way, we may succeed in accomplishing the essential part of our schemes.

9. If, on the other hand, in the midst of difficulties, we are always ready to seize an advantage, we may extricate ourselves from misfortune.

10. Reduce the hostile chiefs by inflicting damage on them; and make trouble for them, and keep them constantly engaged; hold out specious allurements, and make them rush to any given point.

11. *The Art of War* teaches us to rely not on the likelihood of the enemy's not coming, but on our own readiness to receive him; not on the chance of his not attacking, but rather on the fact that we have made our position unassailable.

12. There are five dangerous faults which may affect a general:

    (1) Recklessness, which leads to destruction;

    (2) Cowardice, which leads to capture;

    (3) A hasty temper, which can be provoked by insults;

    (4) A delicacy of honor which is sensitive to shame;

    (5) Over-solicitude for his men, which exposes him to worry and trouble.

13. These are the five besetting sins of a general, ruinous to the conduct of war.

14. When an army is overthrown and its leader slain, the cause will surely be found among these five dangerous faults. Let them be a subject of meditation.

CHAPTER 22

The Army on The March

1. We come now to the question of encamping the army and observing signs of the enemy. Pass quickly over mountains, and keep in the neighborhood of valleys.

2. Camp in high places, facing the sun. Do not climb heights in order to fight. So much for mountain warfare.

3. After crossing a river, you should get far away from it.

4. When an invading force crosses a river in its onward march, do not advance to meet it in midstream. It will be best to let half the army get across, and then deliver your attack

5. If you are anxious to fight, you should not go to meet the invader near a river which he has to cross.

6. Moor your craft higher up than the enemy, and facing the sun. Do not move upstream to meet the enemy. So much for river warfare.

7. In crossing salt-marshes, your sole concern should be to get over them quickly, without any delay.

8. If forced to fight in a salt-marsh, you should have water and grass near you, and get your back to a clump of trees. So much for operations in salt-marshes.

9. In dry, level country, take up an easily accessible position with rising ground to your right and on your rear, so that the danger may be in front, and safety lie behind. So much for campaigning in flat country.

10. These are the four useful branches of military knowledge which enabled the Yellow Emperor to vanquish several sovereigns.

11. All armies prefer high ground to low and sunny places to dark.

12. If you are careful of your men and camp on hard ground, the army will be free from disease of every kind, and this will spell victory.

13. When you come to a hill or a bank, occupy the sunny side, with the slope on your right rear. Thus, you will at once act for the benefit of your soldiers and utilize the natural advantages of the ground.

14. When, in consequence of heavy rains up-country, a river which you wish to ford is swollen and flecked with foam, you must wait until it subsides.

15. A country in which there are precipitous cliffs with torrents running between, deep natural hollows, confined places, tangled thickets, quagmires and crevasses should be left with all possible speed and not approached.

16. While we keep away from such places, we should get the enemy to approach them; while we face them, we should let the enemy have them on his rear.

17. If in the neighborhood of your camp there should be any hilly country, ponds surrounded by aquatic grass, hollow basins filled with reeds, or woods with thick undergrowth, they must be carefully routed out and searched; for these are places where men in ambush or insidious spies are likely to be lurking.

18. When the enemy is close at hand and remains quiet, he is relying on the natural strength of his position.

19. When he keeps aloof and tries to provoke a battle, he is anxious for the other side to advance.

20. If his place of encampment is easy of access, he is tendering a bait.

21. Movement amongst the trees of a forest shows that the enemy is advancing. The appearance of a number of screens in the midst of thick grass means that the enemy wants to make us suspicious.

22. The rising of birds in their flight is the sign of an ambuscade. Startled beasts indicate that a sudden attack is coming.

23. When there is dust rising in a high column, it is the sign of chariots advancing; when the dust is low, but spread over a wide area, it betokens the approach of infantry. When it branches out in different directions, it shows that parties have been sent to collect firewood. A few clouds of dust moving to and fro signify that the army is encamping.

24. Humble words and increased preparations are signs that the enemy is about to advance. Violent language and driving forward as if to the attack are signs that he will retreat.

25. When the light chariots come out first and take up a position on the wings, it is a sign that the enemy is forming for battle.

26. Peace proposals unaccompanied by a sworn covenant indicate a plot.

27. When there is much running about and the soldiers fall into rank, it means that the critical moment has come.

28. When some are seen advancing and some retreating, it is a lure.

29. When the soldiers stand leaning on their spears, they are faint from want of food.

The Army on The March

30. If those who are sent to draw water begin by drinking themselves, the army is suffering from thirst.

31. If the enemy sees an advantage to be gained and makes no effort to secure it, the soldiers are exhausted.

32. If birds gather on any spot, it is unoccupied. Clamor by night betokens nervousness.

33. If there is disturbance in the camp, the general's authority is weak. If the banners and flags are shifted about, sedition is afoot. If the officers are angry, it means that the men are weary.

34. When an army feeds its horses with grain and kills its cattle for food, and when the men do not hang their cooking-pots over the campfires, showing that they will not return to their tents, you may know that they are determined to fight to the death.

35. The sight of men whispering together in small knots or speaking in subdued tones points to disaffection among the rank and file.

36. Too frequent rewards signify that the enemy is at the end of his resources; too many punishments betray a condition of dire distress.

37. To begin by bluster, but afterwards to take fright at the enemy's numbers, shows a supreme lack of intelligence.

38. When envoys are sent with compliments in their mouths, it is a sign that the enemy wishes for a truce.

39. If the enemy's troops march up angrily and remain facing ours for a long time without either joining battle or taking themselves off again, the situation is one that demands great vigilance and circumspection.

40. If our troops are no more in number than the enemy, that is amply sufficient; it means only that no direct attack can be made. What we can do is simply to concentrate all our available strength, keep a close watch on the enemy, and obtain reinforcements.

41. He who exercises no forethought but makes light of his opponents is sure to be captured by them.

42. If soldiers are punished before they have grown attached to you, they will not prove submissive; and, unless submissive, then will be practically useless. If, when the soldiers have become attached to you, punishments are not enforced, they will still be useless.

43. Therefore soldiers must be treated in the first instance with humanity, but kept under control by means of iron discipline. This is a certain road to victory.

44. If in training soldiers' commands are habitually enforced, the army will be well-disciplined; if not, its discipline will be bad.

45. If a general shows confidence in his men but always insists on his orders being obeyed, the gain will be mutual.

CHAPTER 23

Terrain

1. We may distinguish six kinds of terrain:

    (1) Accessible ground

    (2) Entangling ground

    (3) Temporizing ground

    (4) Narrow passes

    (5) Precipitous heights

    (6) Positions at a great distance from the enemy

2. Ground which can be freely traversed by both sides is called accessible.

3. With regard to ground of this nature, be before the enemy in occupying the raised and sunny spots, and carefully guard your line of supplies. Then you will be able to fight with advantage.

4. Ground which can be abandoned but is hard to reoccupy is called entangling.

5. From a position of this sort, if the enemy is unprepared, you may sally forth and defeat him. But if the enemy is prepared for your coming, and you fail to defeat him, then, return being impossible, disaster will ensue.

6. When the position is such that neither side will gain by making the first move, it is called temporizing ground.

7. In a position of this sort, even though the enemy should offer us an attractive bait, it will be advisable not to stir forth, but rather to retreat, thus enticing the enemy in his turn; then, when part of his army has come out, we may deliver our attack with advantage.

8. With regard to narrow passes, if you can occupy them first, let them be strongly garrisoned and await the advent of the enemy.

9. Should the army forestall you in occupying a pass, do not go after him if the pass is fully garrisoned, but only if it is weakly garrisoned.

10. With regard to precipitous heights, if you are beforehand with your adversary, you should occupy the raised and sunny spots, and there wait for him to come up.

11. If the enemy has occupied them before you, do not follow him, but retreat and try to entice him away.

12. If you are situated at a great distance from the enemy, and the strength of the two armies is equal, it is not easy to provoke a battle, and fighting will be to your disadvantage.

13. These six are the principles connected with earth. The general who has attained a responsible post must be careful to study them.

14. Now an army is exposed to six several calamities, not arising from natural causes, but from faults for which the general is responsible. These are as follows:

    (1) Flight

    (2) Insubordination

    (3) Collapse

(4) Ruin

(5) Disorganization

(6) Rout

15. Other conditions being equal, if one force is hurled against another ten times its size, the result will be the flight of the former.

16. When the common soldiers are too strong and their officers too weak, the result is insubordination. When the officers are too strong and the common soldiers too weak, the result is collapse.

17. When the higher officers are angry and insubordinate, and on meeting the enemy give battle on their own account from a feeling of resentment, before the commander-in-chief can tell whether or no he is in a position to fight, the result is ruin.

18. When the general is weak and without authority; when his orders are not clear and distinct; when there are no fixed duties assigned to officers and men, and the ranks are formed in a slovenly haphazard manner, the result is utter disorganization.

19. When a general, unable to estimate the enemy's strength, allows an inferior force to engage a larger one, or hurls a weak detachment against a powerful one, and neglects to place picked soldiers in the front rank, the result must be rout.

20. These are six ways of courting defeat, which must be carefully noted by the general who has attained a responsible post.

21. The natural formation of the country is the soldier's best ally; but a power of estimating the adversary, of controlling

the forces of victory, and of shrewdly calculating difficulties, dangers, and distances constitutes the test of a great general.

22. He who knows these things, and in fighting puts his knowledge into practice, will win his battles. He who knows them not, nor practices them, will surely be defeated.

23. If fighting is sure to result in victory, then you must fight, even though the ruler forbid it; if fighting will not result in victory, then you must not fight even at the ruler's bidding.

24. The general who advances without coveting fame and retreats without fearing disgrace, whose only thought is to protect his country and do good service for his sovereign is the jewel of the kingdom.

25. Regard your soldiers as your children, and they will follow you into the deepest valleys; look upon them as your own beloved sons, and they will stand by you even unto death.

26. If, however, you are indulgent, but unable to make your authority felt; kind-hearted, but unable to enforce your commands; and incapable, moreover, of quelling disorder, then your soldiers must be likened to spoilt children; they are useless for any practical purpose

27. If we know that our own men are in a condition to attack, but are unaware that the enemy is not open to attack, we have gone only halfway towards victory.

28. If we know that the enemy is open to attack, but are unaware that our own men are not in a condition to attack, we have gone only halfway towards victory.

29. If we know that the enemy is open to attack and also know that our men are in a condition to attack, but are unaware that the nature of the ground makes fighting impracticable, we have still gone only halfway towards victory.

30. Hence the experienced soldier, once in motion, is never bewildered; once he has broken camp, he is never at a loss.

31. Hence the saying, "If you know the enemy and know yourself, your victory will not stand in doubt; if you know Heaven and know Earth, you may make your victory complete."

CHAPTER 24

The Nine Situations

1. *The Art of War* recognizes nine varieties of ground:

    (1) Dispersive ground

    (2) Facile ground

    (3) Contentious ground

    (4) Open ground

    (5) Ground of intersecting highways

    (6) Serious ground

    (7) Difficult ground

    (8) Hemmed-in ground

    (9) Desperate ground

2. When a chieftain is fighting in his own territory, it is dispersive ground.

3. When he has penetrated into hostile territory, but to no great distance, it is facile ground.

4. The ground, the possession of which imports great advantage to either side, is contentious ground.

5. The ground on which each side has liberty of movement is open ground.

6. Ground which forms the key to three contiguous states, so that he who occupies it first has most of the empire at his command, is a ground of intersecting highways.

7. When an army has penetrated into the heart of a hostile country, leaving a number of fortified cities in its rear, it is serious ground.

8. Mountain forests, rugged steeps, marshes, and fens—all country that is hard to traverse: this is difficult ground.

9. Ground which is reached through narrow gorges, and from which we can only retire by tortuous paths, so that a small number of the enemy would suffice to crush a large body of our men: this is hemmed-in ground.

10. Ground, on which we can only be saved from destruction by fighting without delay, is desperate ground.

11. On dispersive ground, therefore, fight not. On facile ground, halt not. On contentious ground, attack not.

12. On open ground, do not try to block the enemy's way. On the ground of intersecting highways, join hands with your allies.

13. On serious ground, gather in plunder. In difficult ground, keep steadily on the march.

14. On hemmed-in ground, resort to stratagem. On desperate ground, fight.

15. Those who were called skillful leaders of old knew how to drive a wedge between the enemy's front and rear; to prevent cooperation between his large and small divisions; to hinder the good troops from rescuing the bad, the officers from rallying their men.

16. When the enemy's men were united, they managed to keep them in disorder.

17. When it was to their advantage, they made a forward move; when otherwise, they stopped still.

18. If asked how to cope with a great host of the enemy in orderly array and on the point of marching to the attack, I should say, "Begin by seizing something which your opponent holds dear; then he will be amenable to your will."

19. Rapidity is the essence of war; take advantage of the enemy's unreadiness, make your way by unexpected routes, and attack unguarded spots.

20. The following are the principles to be observed by an invading force: The further you penetrate into a country, the greater will be the solidarity of your troops, and thus the defenders will not prevail against you.

21. Make forays in fertile country in order to supply your army with food.

22. Carefully study the well-being of your men, and do not overtax them. Concentrate your energy and hoard your strength. Keep your army continually on the move, and devise unfathomable plans.

23. Throw your soldiers into positions whence there is no escape, and they will prefer death to flight. If they will face death, there is nothing they may not achieve. Officers and men alike will put forth their uttermost strength.

24. Soldiers when in desperate straits lose the sense of fear. If there is no place of refuge, they will stand firm. If they are in hostile country, they will show a stubborn front. If there is no help for it, they will fight hard.

25. Thus, without waiting to be marshaled, the soldiers will be constantly on the qui vive; without waiting to be asked, they will do your will; without restrictions, they will be faithful; without giving orders, they can be trusted.

The Nine Situations

26. Prohibit the taking of omens, and do away with superstitious doubts. Then, until death itself comes, no calamity need be feared

27. If our soldiers are not overburdened with money, it is not because they have a distaste for riches; if their lives are not unduly long, it is not because they are disinclined to longevity.

28. On the day they are ordered out to battle, your soldiers may weep, those sitting up bedewing their garments, and those lying down letting the tears run down their cheeks. But let them once be brought to bay, and they will display the courage of a Chu or a Kuei.

29. The skillful tactician may be likened to the Shuai-Jan. Now the Shuai-Jan is a snake that is found in the Ch`ang mountains. Strike at its head, and you will be attacked by its tail; strike at its tail, and you will be attacked by its head; strike at its middle, and you will be attacked by head and tail both.

30. Asked if an army can be made to imitate the Shuai-Jan, I should answer, yes. For the men of Wu and the men of Yueh are enemies; yet if they are crossing a river in the same boat and are caught by a storm, they will come to each other's assistance just as the left hand helps the right.

31. Hence it is not enough to put one's trust in the tethering of horses, and the burying of chariot wheels in the ground.

32. The principle on which to manage an army is to set up one standard of courage which all must reach.

33. How to make the best of both strong and weak—that is a question involving the proper use of ground.

34. Thus the skillful general conducts his army just as though he were leading a single man, willy-nilly, by the hand.

35. It is the business of a general to be quiet and thus ensure secrecy; upright and just, and thus maintain order.

36. He must be able to mystify his officers and men by false reports and appearances, and thus keep them in total ignorance.

37. By altering his arrangements and changing his plans, he keeps the enemy without definite knowledge. By shifting his camp and taking circuitous routes, he prevents the enemy from anticipating his purpose.

38. At the critical moment, the leader of an army acts like one who has climbed up a height and then kicks away the ladder behind him. He carries his men deep into hostile territory before he shows his hand.

39. He burns his boats and breaks his cooking-pots; like a shepherd driving a flock of sheep, he drives his men this way and that, and nothing knows whither he is going.

40. To muster his host and bring it into danger—this may be termed the business of the general.

41. The different measures suited to the nine varieties of ground, the expediency of aggressive or defensive tactics, and the fundamental laws of human nature—these are things that must most certainly be studied.

42. When invading hostile territory, the general principle is that penetrating deeply brings cohesion; penetrating but a short way means dispersion.

43. When you leave your own country behind and take your army across the neighboring territory, you find yourself on

critical ground. When there are means of communication on all four sides, the ground is one of intersecting highways.

44. When you penetrate deeply into a country, it is serious ground. When you penetrate but a little way, it is facile ground.

45. When you have the enemy's strongholds on your rear and narrow passes in front, it is hemmed-in ground. When there is no place of refuge at all, it is desperate ground.

46. Therefore, on dispersive ground, I would inspire my men with unity of purpose. On facile ground, I would see that there is close connection between all parts of my army.

47. On contentious ground, I would hurry up my rear.

48. On open ground, I would keep a vigilant eye on my defences. On ground of intersecting highways, I would consolidate my alliances.

49. On serious ground, I would try to ensure a continuous stream of supplies. On difficult ground, I would keep pushing on along the road.

50. On hemmed-in ground, I would block any way of retreat.

51. For it is the soldier's disposition to offer an obstinate resistance when surrounded, to fight hard when he cannot help himself, and to obey promptly when he has fallen into danger.

52. We cannot enter into alliance with neighboring princes until we are acquainted with their designs. We are not fit to lead an army on the march unless we are familiar with the face of the country—its mountains and forests, its pitfalls and precipices, its marshes and swamps. We shall be unable to turn natural advantages to account unless we make use of local guides.

53. To be ignorant of any one of the following four or five principles does not befit a warlike prince.

54. When a warlike prince attacks a powerful state, his generalship shows itself in preventing the concentration of the enemy's forces. He overawes his opponents, and their allies are prevented from joining against him.

55. Hence he does not strive to ally himself with all and sundry, nor does he foster the power of other states. He carries out his own secret designs, keeping his antagonists in awe. Thus he is able to capture their cities and overthrow their kingdoms.

56. Bestow rewards without regard to rule, issue orders without regard to previous arrangements, and you will be able to handle a whole army as though you had to do with but a single man.

57. Confront your soldiers with the deed itself; never let them know your design. When the outlook is bright, bring it before their eyes, but tell them nothing when the situation is gloomy.

58. Place your army in deadly peril, and it will survive; plunge it into desperate straits, and it will come off in safety.

59. For it is precisely when a force has fallen into harm's way that it is capable of striking a blow for victory.

60. Success in warfare is gained by carefully accommodating ourselves to the enemy's purpose.

61. By persistently hanging on the enemy's flank, we shall succeed in the long run in killing the commander-in-chief.

62. This is called ability to accomplish a thing by sheer cunning.

63. On the day that you take up your command, block the frontier passes, destroy the official tallies, and stop the passage of all emissaries.

64. Be stern in the council-chamber, so that you may control the situation.

65. If the enemy leaves a door open, you must rush in.

66. Forestall your opponent by seizing what he holds dear, and subtly contrive to time his arrival on the ground.

67. Walk in the path defined by rule, and accommodate yourself to the enemy until you can fight a decisive battle.

68. At first, then, exhibit the coyness of a maiden, until the enemy gives you an opening; afterwards, emulate the rapidity of a running hare, and it will be too late for the enemy to oppose you.

CHAPTER 25

The Attack by Fire

1. Sun Tzu said: There are five ways of attacking with fire. The first is to burn soldiers in their camp; the second is to burn stores; the third is to burn baggage trains; the fourth is to burn arsenals and magazines; the fifth is to hurl dropping fire among the enemy.

2. In order to carry out an attack, we must have means available; the material for raising fire should always be kept in readiness.

3. There is a proper season for making attacks with fire, and special days for starting a conflagration.

4. The proper season is when the weather is very dry; the special days are those when the moon is in the constellations of the Sieve, the Wall, the Wing, or the Cross-bar, for these four are all days of rising wind.

5. In attacking with fire, one should be prepared to meet five possible developments:

    (1) When fire breaks out inside to enemy's camp, respond at once with an attack from without.

    (2) If there is an outbreak of fire, but the enemy's soldiers remain quiet, bide your time and do not attack.

    (3) When the force of the flames has reached its height, follow it up with an attack if that is practicable; if not, stay where you are.

The Attack by Fire

(4) If it is possible to make an assault with fire from without, do not wait for it to break out within, but deliver your attack at a favorable moment.

(5) When you start a fire, be to windward of it. Do not attack from the leeward.

6. A wind that rises in the daytime lasts long, but a night breeze soon falls.

7. In every army, the five developments connected with fire must be known, the movements of the stars calculated, and a watch kept for the proper days.

8. Hence those who use fire as an aid to the attack show intelligence; those who use water as an aid to the attack gain an accession of strength.

9. By means of water, an enemy may be intercepted, but not robbed of all his belongings.

10. Unhappy is the fate of one who tries to win his battles and succeed in his attacks without cultivating the spirit of enterprise; for the result is wasted time and general stagnation.

11. Hence the saying: The enlightened ruler lays his plans well ahead; the good general cultivates his resources.

12. Move not unless you see an advantage; use not your troops unless there is something to be gained; fight not unless the position is critical.

13. No ruler should put troops into the field merely to gratify his own spleen; no general should fight a battle simply out of pique.

14. If it is to your advantage, make a forward move; if not, stay where you are.

15. Anger may in time change to gladness; vexation may be succeeded by contentment.

16. But a kingdom that has once been destroyed can never come again into being; nor can the dead ever be brought back to life.

17. Hence the enlightened ruler is heedful, and the good general full of caution. This is the way to keep a country at peace and an army intact.

CHAPTER 26

The Use of Spies

1. Raising a host of a hundred thousand men and marching them great distances entails heavy loss on the people and a drain on the resources of the state. The daily expenditure will amount to a thousand ounces of silver. There will be commotion at home and abroad, and men will drop down exhausted on the highways. As many as seven hundred thousand families will be impeded in their labor.

2. Hostile armies may face each other for years, striving for the victory which is decided in a single day. This being so, to remain in ignorance of the enemy's condition simply because one grudges the outlay of a hundred ounces of silver in honors and emoluments is the height of inhumanity.

3. One who acts thus is no leader of men, no present help to his sovereign, and no master of victory.

4. Thus, what enables the wise sovereign and the good general to strike and conquer, and to achieve things beyond the reach of ordinary men, is foreknowledge.

5. Now this foreknowledge cannot be elicited from spirits; it cannot be obtained inductively from experience, nor by any deductive calculation.

6. Knowledge of the enemy's dispositions can only be obtained from other men.

7. Hence the use of spies, of whom there are five classes:

(1) Local spies

(2) Inward spies

(3) Converted spies

(4) Doomed spies

(5) Surviving spies.

8. When these five kinds of spies are all at work, none can discover the secret system. This is called "divine manipulation of the threads." It is the sovereign's most precious faculty.

9. Having local spies means employing the services of the inhabitants of a district.

10. Having inward spies, making use of officials of the enemy.

11. Having converted spies, getting hold of the enemy's spies and using them for our own purposes.

12. Having doomed spies, doing certain things openly for purposes of deception, and allowing our spies to know of them and report them to the enemy.

13. Surviving spies, finally, are those who bring back news from the enemy's camp.

14. Hence, intimate relations are to be maintained with none in the whole army more than with spies. None should be more liberally rewarded. In no other business should greater secrecy be preserved.

15. Spies cannot be usefully employed without a certain intuitive sagacity.

16. They cannot be properly managed without benevolence and straightforwardness.

17. Without subtle ingenuity of mind, one cannot make certain of the truth of their reports.

18. Be subtle! Be subtle! And use your spies for every kind of business.

19. If a secret piece of news is divulged by a spy before the time is ripe, he must be put to death together with the man to whom the secret was told.

20. Whether the object be to crush an army, to storm a city, or to assassinate an individual, it is always necessary to begin by finding out the names of the attendants, the aides-de- camp, and the doorkeepers and sentries of the general in command. Our spies must be commissioned to ascertain these.

21. The enemy's spies who have come to spy on us must be sought out, tempted with bribes, led away and comfortably housed. Thus they will become converted spies and available for our service.

22. It is through the information brought by the converted spy that we are able to acquire and employ local and inward spies.

23. It is owing to his information, again, that we can cause the doomed spy to carry false tidings to the enemy.

24. Lastly, it is by his information that the surviving spy can be used on appointed occasions.

25. The end and aim of spying in all its five varieties is knowledge of the enemy; and this knowledge can only be derived, in the first instance, from the converted spy. Hence it is essential that the converted spy be treated with the utmost liberality.

26. Of old, the rise of the Yin dynasty who had served under the Hsia. Likewise, the rise of the Chou dynasty was due to Lu Ya, who had served under the Yin.

27. Hence it is only the enlightened ruler and the wise general who will use the highest intelligence of the army for purposes of spying and thereby they achieve great results. Spies are a most important element in water, because on them depends an army's ability to move.

Afterward

Discovery is a journey.

A journey is discovery.

Sometimes you begin to discover, when you start the journey. One discovery leads to another one, creating a chain of profound experiences and insights that keep inspiring you for a lifetime.

Sun Tzu's thoughts fascinated me, and this book was born. As I was finishing it, slowly the realization became loud. That, Sun Tzu's ideas are much more meaningful, than this book offers and the essence of *The Art of War* has potential to provide deeper insights to the project management community. A comparison of the PMBOK® with *The Art of War* is irresistible but not enough to leverage the wisdom of Sun Tzu.

I believe that the insights from eternal ancient texts like *The Art of War*, can help us in our daily life, both work and personal life. Therefore, after careful thought, I decided to organize the key learnings from *The Art of War* into two more books, each covering project management from different perspectives.

Let me finish this book by saying, *to be continued...*

www.ingramcontent.com/pod-product-compliance
Lightning Source LLC
Chambersburg PA
CBHW071522180526
45171CB00002B/351